The Manasseh Effect
SECOND EDITION
The History of Tomorrow
John J. Higgins
Josiah Publications • Phoenix, Arizona

About the book
The Manasseh Effect testifies of the far-reaching consequences of sin. King Manasseh's actions foreshadow the coming age of the Antichrist and his dealings with Israel. His actions in the past set in motion a series of judgments that will change the world.

Josiah Publications
For information on this and other Biblical studies, please contact us:

Josiah Publications
P.O. Box 51207
Phoenix, AZ 85076
480-345-6200
www.TheHistoryOfTomorrow.com
www.InTheDays.com
www.RadioFreeChurch.com
www.JesusLifeAndMinistry.com
www.ITDStore.com

Initially transcribed by Cindy Scinto.
Cover, Text Design, and Editing: Shauna Higgins, Gary and Louise Smith.

ISBN 13: 978-0-9793653-0-0
ISBN 10: 0-9793653-0-9

1 2 3 4 5 6 7 8 9 MG 15 14 13 12 11 10 09 08 07

If you would like a copy of this book and can't afford it, contact us and we'll send you one at no charge. You can read this book online and download the accompanying chart at www.TheHistoryOfTomorrow.com.

Dedication

I want to thank my Lord Jesus for the wisdom and strength to continue in the faith and write these words.

I'm also thankful for my wife, Shauna and our children Jamie, Seth, Jeremy, Adam, and Tamara, who have been a joy to our lives and a hope for the future. Many a day they have allowed me to work late and leave early in the morning to continue this endeavor. When I wanted to give up I was encouraged to go on. What a wonderful family—I am truly blessed.

Acknowledgments

I want to thank Pastor Chuck Smith and his wife Kay for their years of faithfulness to God's Word. Next, I want to thank John and Cindy Scinto, old friends that helped with the first publishing, and Gary and Louise Smith, who have been used by our Lord to inspire the re-write and distribution of this endeavor. My wife's parents, Mart and Vida, have always encouraged us to carry on. Dr. Robert Ward, a friend and board member has also contributed to our joy in this labor.

If this book bears any fruit, I know many who will share in the rewards when Jesus returns. Please be aware that we believe that the only book necessary for spiritual growth and fellowship with God is the Bible. If you take the time to read this, please do not neglect your own studies of His Word. The thoughts presented in this writing are based upon the fundamental truths of God's Word and some theories of the writer. If any conflict arises, always return to His Word for safety.

How to use this book

How the chart and the book work together

The Manasseh Effect comes with a chart. If you need a chart, you can download an Acrobat version that you can print from www.TheHistoryOfTomorrow.com.

There are boxed letters (**A**)in the text of the book that correspond to locations on the chart. So as you read, you can refer to the chart to better understand the events discussed. In Appendix A, there is a list of all the boxed letter references and where to find them in the text. This enables you to find where the references are in the book if you are starting from the chart.

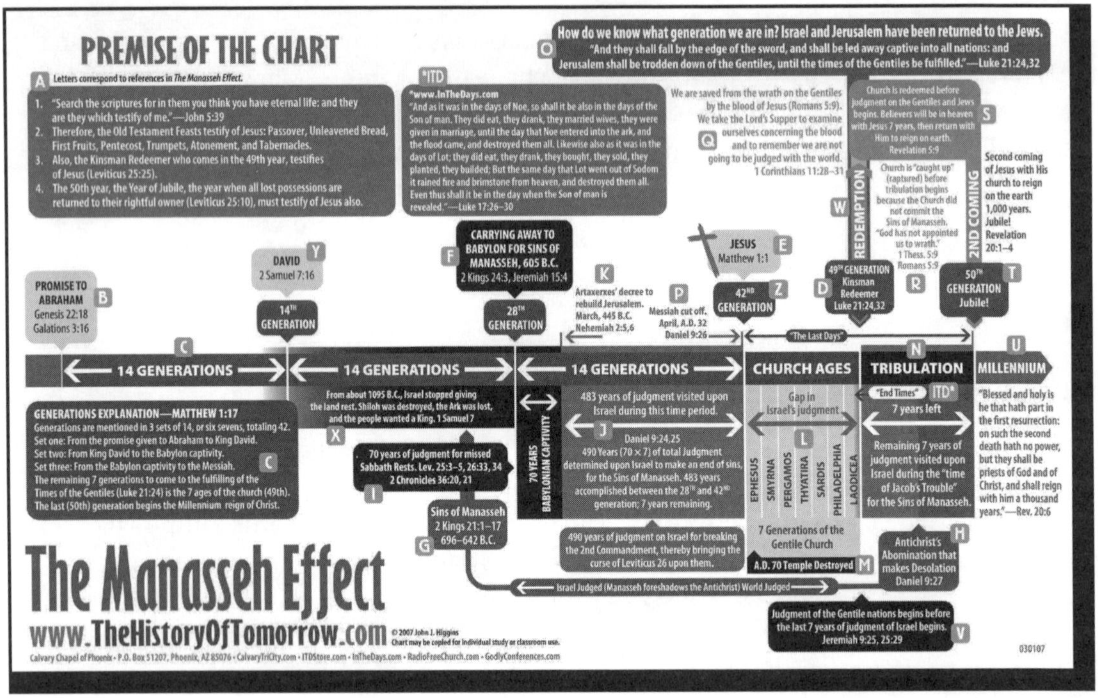

Don't take our word for it—Be a Berean Christian

In the book of Acts, Paul commends the Berean Christians.

"These were more noble than those in Thessalonica, in that they received the word with all readiness of mind, and *searched the scriptures daily, whether those things were so."—Acts 17:11*

Be as the Bereans were. Search these things out in the scriptures for yourself.

Preface

We are all instructed to study to show ourselves approved unto God (2 Timothy 2:15). The scripture also states that knowledge puffs up, but that charity edifies (1 Corinthians 8:1). Therefore, I believe we should study God's Word and that study should lead us to His love as described in 1 Corinthians chapter 13.

In 1 John 3:16 we find that when we grasp the extent of His love for us, it will lead us to lay down our lives for our brethren. This love does not exalt itself over others, but causes us to put the needs of others above our own needs.

In the beginning of our Lord's third year of ministry (John 7:10 through 10:21), after He had been rejected by the Sanhedrin, Jesus departed Jerusalem, and journeyed into the countryside around Judea. At this time our Lord appointed His 70 elders. This is recorded in Luke chapters 10–13.

Since the spiritual shepherds (Jewish leaders) in Jerusalem rejected the Good Shepherd, Jesus anointed the 70 men he had appointed and sent them to care for the lost sheep of Judah (Luke chapter 10).

The 70 went to God's sheep in Israel, but when they returned they exalted themselves because of the knowledge and power they had received from Jesus' anointing. Jesus recognized their attitude and instructed the elders to look towards heaven for their fame and not to this earth. Then Jesus prayed.

"…I thank thee, O Father, Lord of heaven and earth, that thou hast hid these things from the wise and prudent, and hast revealed them unto babes: even so, Father; for so it seemed good in thy sight."—*Luke 10:21*

Jesus went on to teach these men that the power and revelation they had just received was from Him and was given to reveal His Father to them and to this world.

"All things are delivered to me of my Father: and no man knoweth who the Son is, but the Father; and who the Father is, but the Son, and he to whom the Son will reveal him."—*Luke 10:22*

Taking the men aside, Jesus told them how blessed they were to know and experience these things that prophets and kings throughout the ages had desired to know (Luke 10:24).

The Manasseh Effect is about our Father's plan for the believers throughout the ages. I am a student of Jesus and not a scholar. There is only one scholar and that is Jesus.

I am not an authority of Greek or Hebrew. Knowledge of the original languages is useful in study, but it never makes the knowledge that has been delivered to us any less inspired.

I am a Gentile that has been given the inspired Word of God in English. I know that the Lord is able to communicate His inerrant message to the English speaking people in their own language.

Our studies of God's Word are to humble us to serve, not to rejoice in our knowledge. This book is not designed to give us secret knowledge that will exalt us over others. I have no knowledge that can not be found by anyone who reads and compares scripture with scripture. I am a student that gives himself to reading the Word of God. Please remember that knowledge puffs up and charity strengthens.—*John Higgins*

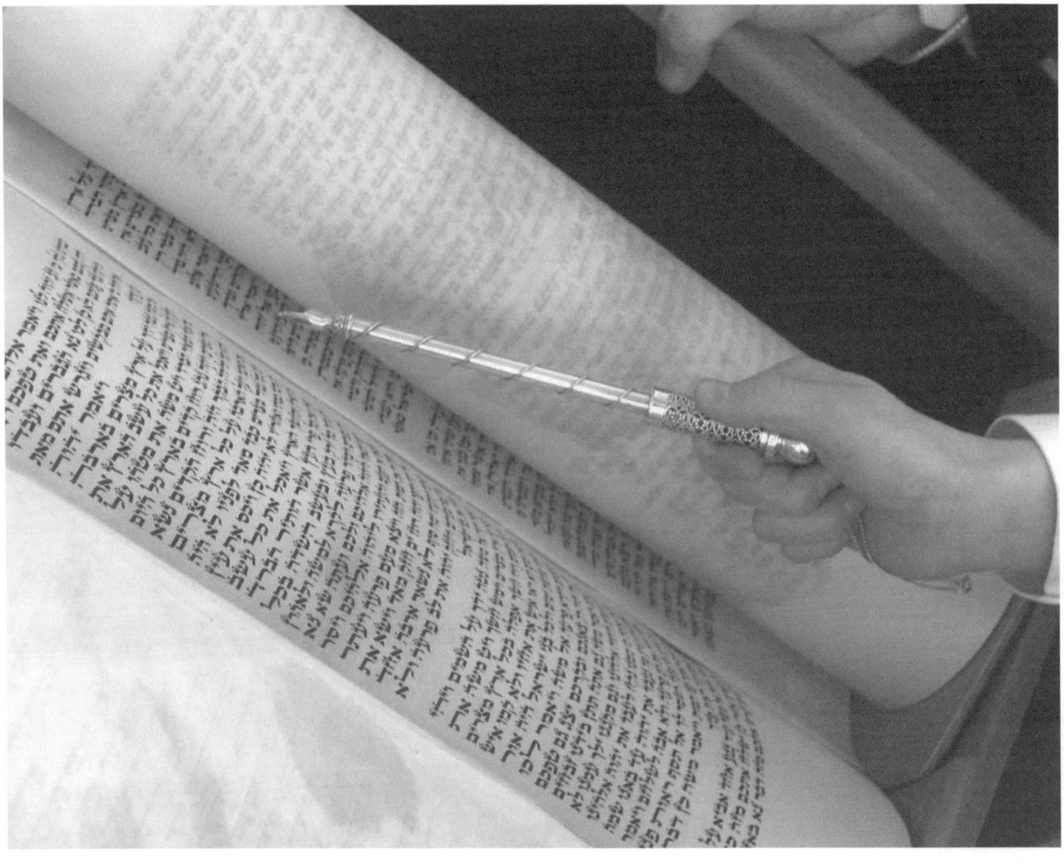

Contents

Introduction 1

1. The Foundation—All Scripture Testifies of Jesus 5
2. The Promise 9
3. Generations 11
4. The Result of Sin 19
5. Cause of Remaining Judgment 27
6. Judgment 35
7. The Church Age 47
8. The Last Generation 55
9. Deliverance 65
10. Order of Things 73
11. With All His Saints 77
12. Conclusion 83
13. Where are you in all of this? 91

Addendum—Which Bible? 95

Appendix A—Chart-to-Book References 100

Appendix B—Nuclear Proliferation Chart 101

Scripture Index 102

Index 105

Read Through the Bible in One Year 111

Jesus' Life and Ministry FREE Bible School Course 114

In The Days and Radio Free Church Websites 116

In The Days Bookstore Study Resources 118

"Because he hath appointed a day, in the which he will judge the world in righteousness by that man whom he hath ordained; whereof he hath given assurance unto all men, in that he hath raised him from the dead."—*Acts 17:31*

Introduction: Early Beginnings

Do you know what your appointment with destiny is? How do you see God stepping into your life and when do you think He will? Have you ever stopped to consider that your personal destiny is intricately involved with events that took place thousands of years ago? We will attempt to answer these puzzling questions throughout the pages of this book.

The Ordained Judge

The scriptures clearly state that Paul (first on Mars Hill, and later before King Agrippa), explained why the Holy Spirit sent the apostles and their followers to the Gentile nations. Through the centuries this mission has been redefined by the ruling powers in Christianity, but the reason Paul was to preach to the Gentiles remains the same.

"To open their eyes, and to turn them from darkness to light, and from the power of Satan unto God."—*Acts 26:18*

Paul told the Gentiles to turn from their idols and Satan to the Living God.

"And the times of this ignorance God winked at; but now commandeth all men every where to repent: Because he hath appointed a day, in the which he will judge the world in righteousness by *that man* whom he hath ordained; whereof he hath given assurance unto all men, in that he hath raised him from the dead."—*Acts 17:30,31*

As believers, we know *that man* is Jesus our Lord and Saviour. Paul didn't tell everyone that the message of the Saviour would create a perfect society. He did not imply that it would develop into a conservative movement, or that through a dominating system of government that would be called "democracy," life would be great, and peace would come to the earth.

To the contrary, the scriptures declare that the fury, wrath, and anger of God has not been seen by mankind since the days of Noah. God's Word says that all of mankind will behold His wrath fully in the latter times (Jeremiah 23:20 and 30:24). N

Both Old Testament prophets Jeremiah and Ezekiel, in separate visions, beheld the fury of God's wrath poured out upon the world. If this fury has been reserved until the End Times, and if these can be proven to be those days, then we should expect this fury to be revealed soon. The Gospel's outreach to the Gentile nations and the subsequent call to repentance therefore will enable those that repent to escape this fury. ITD

Paul wrote to the Romans and the Thessalonians to tell them they could escape the wrath of God because of the blood of Jesus that was shed for them. *The Manasseh Effect* is about the intricacies of that escape and the certainty of the wrath to come upon Israel and the Gentile nations. S V

Tepid Christianity

The teaching of the deliverance of believers from God's wrath is being cast aside in these days of increasingly tepid Christianity. In order to have large followings and organizations, the modern church has developed programs to keep people involved long-term.

It's difficult to encourage people to dedicate time and resources to large building programs if they believe Jesus will cast the new building to the ground in the near future. It's hard to get people to concentrate on issues of church growth, building organizations, or long-term programs if repentance is preached as the means of escape and the imminent return of Jesus Christ is foremost on their minds.

In order to persuade people to finance ten- or twenty-year programs up front, visionaries need people to catch their vision. Many modern church leaders fear that the scriptural teaching of the imminent return of Christ and world judgment would certainly deter people from going along with their agendas.

Many of today's growth-oriented churches even discourage the study of the book of Revelation or any prophecy from the Bible. They tell their congregations that the study of prophecy is a waste of time even though about fifty percent of the Bible is made up of prophecy.

Although every generation needed to be ready for His coming, I believe the current generation has the greatest chance of seeing that event. My hope is that the teachings presented in this book will cause the reader to seek the truth, to return to the early beginnings of the church, and see if the Bible's warnings to the final generation are being fulfilled.

The Question

In 1973, during the Yom Kippur War, the question was asked of me, "Why are we happy that the Arabs are being killed and Jews are killing them? Aren't we concerned that both groups are going to Hell?"

With this question on my mind and in my heart, I decided to re-read the Old and New Testaments to seek an answer. I wanted to take a fresh look at what I had been taught in the church to see if it was true.

It was during this search that I came to a Biblical understanding concerning the reason Israel was in existence today and how this relates to the church. In 1978, when I shared my findings to groups of brethren, the responses ranged from, "What a revelation!" to "You are teaching falsely!"

Because of the division, over the next fifteen years I concentrated on teaching the simpler things of the Gospel while continuing to study and test my beliefs about how Israel relates to the church.

Bulgarian Christians

While in Austria in July of 1993, I spoke to a group of Bulgarian believers. One of their Pastors asked me to teach on the subject of the End Times out of the Old Testament. Pastor Al James, my close friend and collaborator on this trip, was teaching from the New Testament book of Timothy. I thought to myself, "Teach from the Old Testament? I came prepared for something else." ITD

Then I considered the subject I had taught recently at home about the different types and figures of Jesus Christ which are found in the book of Exodus. There are many types and figures of the Second Coming and the deliverance of the believers from God's judgment in the books of the Pentateuch.

As I taught the second night's study on the End Times, the very first question I posed to the congregation was whether or not they believed in the Biblical principal of the deliverance of the believer from God's judgment. When dealing with people from another land and another culture, you don't always know how well versed they are in God's Word. I wanted to be sensitive to their beliefs and find out where I needed to begin.

They answered readily that they believed in this doctrine. This opened the way for my response that I believed this event would take place before the last seven years of Earth History. S W

"So do most of us," they replied. Their answer was confident. I found this astonishing considering these Bulgarian believers had not been able to listen to many American preachers for at least the last seventy years. They had obtained this knowledge directly from the Bible. With little or no communication with the Western World, they had an understanding that was compatible with mine.

As I continued to share my beliefs that night, they became so excited that they asked me to continue with the study throughout the week long conference. The next day they asked me to illustrate the study on a chalkboard, which they copied.

This inspired me to spend my free time on the computer redesigning the chart to help facilitate its distribution. How inspiring it was to see the excitement the Bulgarian believers manifested over a principle that is so readily shunned in the USA. It was this excitement that prompted me to put on paper the understanding that I believe the Lord had given me.

At that point in my life, I had been in ministry full time for over twenty-five years, and the need to write a book had never struck me before. However, with hopelessness developing in our rapidly deteriorating society, and with sin and false doctrine abounding, I became inspired to communicate God's plan for His church in writing. My desire is that the reader of this book will find again the blessed hope of the early church, rekindling the desire to serve Jesus.

The Puzzle

The chapters start off methodically with basic Biblical principles that must be grasped in order to see the full extent of our prophetic destiny.

Each chapter contains a piece of the puzzle. When the puzzle is completed, we will be able to see a complete picture of our destiny—*The History of Tomorrow.*

The Manasseh Effect studies the light of God's deliverance revealing the meaning behind the shadowed truths of the Old Testament.

From the Author

If you find anything in this book to be true, that's the Holy Spirit. If you find anything in this book to be false, that's me.

"And many false prophets shall rise, and shall deceive many."—*Matthew 24:11*

Chapter 1: The Foundational Truth—All Scripture Testifies of Jesus

The foundational truth for this book is that all Bible scripture testifies of Jesus Christ. A

"Search the scriptures; for in them ye think ye have eternal life: and they are they which testify of me."—*John 5:39*

This truth is illustrated by the use of scriptural principles. At this point it is very important for the reader to take the time to establish in his own mind some of the basic principles that form this foundation.

Truth: Jesus is the Passover Lamb

The first principle is that the scriptures testify of Jesus in many different ways. For instance, in the book of John, John the Baptist identifies Jesus as the Lamb of God.

"...Behold the Lamb of God, which taketh away the sin of the world."—*John 1:29*

The next principle is that the Old Testament shows that a lamb was slain at Passover. The very first Passover was instituted when God commanded his people who were captive in Egypt, to kill a lamb and mark their door posts with its blood.

"For the LORD will pass through to smite the Egyptians; and when he seeth the blood upon the lintel, and on the two side posts, the LORD will pass over the door, and *will not suffer the destroyer* to come in unto your houses to smite you."—*Exodus 12:23*

Only the people with the blood of the lamb on their door posts were spared. That blood represented (foreshadowed) the blood of Jesus Christ, for He is the Lamb of God. This New Testament scripture designates Jesus Christ as the Passover Lamb.

"...For even *Christ our passover* is sacrificed for us."—*1 Corinthians 5:7*

The Lamb that was slain in the Old Testament was an illustration, foreshadow, or type of Jesus Christ. The lamb slain testified of what Christ would do—shed His blood upon the cross to free us from bondage and keep us from death. *The destroyer, Satan, can not harm us* because we are covered by the blood of the Lamb—by the blood of Jesus Christ.

The Heavenly High Priest and the Heavenly Temple.

In Hebrews 8:1–4 and 10:12–13, Jesus is depicted as a High Priest who sits at the right hand of the throne of God. He is proclaimed by the writer of Hebrews to be a Minister of the sanctuary and the *true* Tabernacle which was erected by God, not man.

Therefore, if there is a *true* Tabernacle (Temple) erected by God, then there must have been a Temple erected by man that was merely a representation, or type, of the true Temple. The verses in Hebrews 8:1–4 also state that if Jesus was on earth, He would not be a priest because earthly priests offer gifts according to *the Law.*

The Law: A Shadow

When Moses spoke with God on the mountain and received the instructions known as *The Law*, he received a blueprint of what Jesus would accomplish for us. The Law and its instruments are declared in Hebrews to be types and figures of the Heavenly Temple, and the Heavenly High Priest.

"Who serve unto the example and *shadow of heavenly things*, as Moses was admonished of God when he was about to make the tabernacle: for, See, saith he, that thou make all things according to the *pattern* shewed to thee in the mount."—*Hebrews 8:5*

Therefore, when Moses constructed the Ark of the Covenant, he made an object that represented Christ with all His earthly and heavenly ministry embodied within its design.

The Law of Moses wasn't given to make us perfect. It was written to show mankind what Jesus would do and how He would make peace with God for us. This is verified in Hebrews.

"For the *law* having a *shadow of good things to come*, and not the very image of the things, *can never* with those sacrifices which they offered year by year continually make the comers thereunto perfect."—*Hebrews 10:1*

The Sacrifice

The blood atonement in the Old Testament is called a pattern in the New Testament.

"And almost all things are by the law purged with blood; and without shedding of blood is no remission. It was therefore necessary that the *patterns of things in the heavens* should be purified with these…"—*Hebrews 9:22, 23*

"For the life of the flesh is in the blood: and I have given it to you upon the altar to make an atonement for your souls: for it is the blood that maketh an atonement for the soul." —*Leviticus 17:11*

When Moses sprinkled the book and the ark with the blood of animals, he was showing what Christ would do for us through His shed blood on the cross.

One example of this, called the *Law of The Red Heifer*, is found in the book of Numbers chapter 19. During this ceremony, the priest killed a heifer and then burned it down to ashes. The ashes were mixed with water and sprinkled on the people. This was supposed to remove the sins of their flesh and purify it before God. Their sins weren't purged by the heifer; it was merely a cow which had been killed and used for the ceremony.

So this ceremony, a shadow of heavenly truth, represented Jesus Christ and how he would die for us. His blood was mixed with water as it came out of his side, thereby establishing that the heifer was a type of Christ. The sprinkling of the blood and the heifer ceremony revealed that Jesus Christ would take away all the sins of the world and purify our flesh before God.

"It was therefore necessary that the patterns of things in the heavens should be purified with these; but the heavenly things themselves with better sacrifices than these."—*Hebrews 9:23*

So the blood of animals such as bulls, goats, lambs, and others can never take away sin. These sacrifices were there to show that *only* Christ can take away the sins of the world and drive the wicked one, Satan, from the heavens.

Truth: All Scripture is Prophecy

We started this chapter noting that all scripture testifies of Jesus.

"Search the scriptures… and they are they which testify of me."—*John 5:39*

In Revelation 22:8, John the apostle falls down and starts to worship the angel that showed him the visions. The angel tells John not to worship him, but to worship God, and adds:

"…for the testimony of Jesus is the spirit of prophecy."—*Revelation 19:10*

Here's an important truth. Taking the very words of Jesus, and the words of the angel, only one conclusion can be drawn: if every scripture testifies of Jesus, and the testimony of Jesus is the Spirit of Prophecy, *then all scripture is prophecy*.

These truths applied practically

When someone comes to you with another book and encourages you to read it explaining that it is another testament, you can tell them what the scriptures state in Revelation.

"For I testify unto every man that heareth the words of the prophecy of this book, If any man shall add unto these things, God shall add unto him the plagues that are written in this book: And if any man shall take away from the words of the book of this prophecy, God shall take away his part out of the book of life, and out of the holy city, and from the things which are written in this book."—*Revelation 22:18, 19*

They may reply with the defense that they have not added words to *The Book* but that they have *another* testament. These are the defenses of those who explain that Revelation 22:18 *only refers to the book of Revelation*. Their inaccuracy is exposed by the scriptures themselves.

"Ye shall not add unto the word which I command you, neither shall ye diminish ought from it, that ye may keep the commandments of the LORD your God which I command you."
—*Deuteronomy 4:2*

"What thing soever I command you, observe to do it: thou shalt not add thereto, nor diminish from it."—*Deuteronomy 12:32*

"Every word of God is pure: he is a shield unto them that put their trust in him. Add thou not unto his words, lest he reprove thee, and thou be found a liar."—*Proverbs 30:6*

So you see, we are prevented from adding anything to the entire Old Testament. The word *prophecy* as used in Revelation 22:18 refers to the words of the entire Bible. Remember, all scripture testifies of Christ and the testimony of Jesus is the spirit of prophecy, making all scripture prophecy.

If you add anything, anywhere to scripture, you are adding to the *whole* of the scripture and thereby are trying to add to the word of the prophecy of this Book.

So, those who proclaim *another* testament—who counsel you to read and study it because they received it from an angel—are in error. Turn away from the temptation and curiosity to read the heresy they dangle in front of you.

I knew of a young man of sixteen who was a new believer. He had recently left a group in which he was taught to read *another testament* along with the Bible. They considered it crucial because it had been given to them by an angel. He replied to the group with childlike innocence, "But it says in the book of Revelation that if I add anything to this book (the Bible) all the plagues shall be added to me and if I take away anything from this book, my name will be taken out of the Book of Life. Does this book which you say was given to your church by an angel add anything to the Bible?"

The leader answered, "No, son, it does not add anything at all."

"Well then does it take away anything? he asked.

"No, son, it does not take away anything," the leader replied.

"If it doesn't take away anything nor does it add to the Bible, then why would I need it?" asked the boy earnestly.

Out of the mouths of babes comes perfect praise! That's absolutely true. Why would you need something that doesn't add or take away from the Word of God? These people presenting *another* Gospel will always tell you it doesn't add or take away. They don't want to admit that they could be at risk of failure or punishment. These kinds of counterfeit works are sufficiently persuasive to deceive the very elect, if it were possible (Matthew 24:24). Run from them!

These people are false teachers. Jesus prophesied that there would be an increase of such people just before His Second Coming (Matthew 24:11). Now is the time to be looking for the return of Jesus.

"Wherefore when he cometh into the world, he saith, Sacrifice and offering thou wouldest not, but a body hast thou prepared me: In burnt offerings and sacrifices for sin thou hast had no pleasure. Then said I, Lo, I come (in the volume of the book it is written of me,) to do thy will, O God."
—Hebrews 10:5–7

Chapter 2: The Promise

The promise is simple.
It started with God's promise to Abraham.

"And in thy *seed* shall all the nations of the earth be blessed; because thou hast obeyed my voice."*—Genesis 22:18* B

The New Testament book of Galatians says that Jesus Christ is the seed referred to in Genesis 22.

"Now to Abraham and his seed were the promises made. He saith not, And to seeds, as of many; but as of one, And to thy seed, which is Christ."*—Galatians 3:16* E

As for me, I have chosen to believe the Bible. Jesus Christ is the seed promised to Abraham!

"The book of the generation of Jesus Christ, the son of David, the son of Abraham. (*Here He starts with the Promise.)* Abraham begat Isaac; and Isaac begat Jacob; and Jacob begat Judas and his brethren; And Judas begat…"
—Matthew 1:1–3

The genealogy of Abraham follows through Ruth and Boaz, Jesse and King David, and onto Solomon. Matthew brings the lineage all the way to Joseph, the husband of Mary. Y

"And Jacob begat Joseph the husband of Mary, of whom was born Jesus, who is called Christ."*—Matthew 1:16*

That is *the Promise* to Abraham, the nations, and the whole earth. Jesus Christ was the fulfillment of the Promise to Abraham. B E

"And thou shalt number seven sabbaths of years unto thee, seven times seven years; and the space of the seven sabbaths of years shall be unto thee forty and nine years. Then shalt thou cause the trumpet of the jubile to sound on the tenth day of the seventh month, in the day of atonement…"—*Leviticus 25:8, 9*

Chapter 3: Generations

Matthew chapter 1 states that all the generations from Abraham to David number fourteen. There are also fourteen generations from David to the carrying away of the Children of Israel to Babylon, and fourteen from the carrying away to the birth of Jesus Christ. C

"So all the generations from Abraham to David are fourteen generations; and from David until the carrying away into Babylon are fourteen generations; and from the carrying away into Babylon unto Christ are fourteen generations. Now the birth of Jesus Christ was on this wise…"—*Matthew 1:17, 18*

As I studied these scriptures over the years, I was fascinated at the separation of fourteen generations between such marked events. I read this chapter in Matthew before I became a Christian, and even then I could see that the three separations of fourteen generational periods were emphasized. They were important enough that God ushered in the birth of Christ with the knowledge that there were these three sets of fourteen.

Jesus Christ was born in the forty-second generation from the promise given to Abraham. For many years the significance of this fact eluded me. Z

However, I did realize that in forty-two, there are six sevens. There are two sevens between Abraham and David and two sevens between David and the carrying away to Babylon, and two sevens from the carrying away to Babylon to Christ. The number seven is found frequently in the Bible, and I became interested in this pattern.

The puzzle begins

I read through the Bible many times. Slowly, after several years of study, I began to get the picture of its entirety. Imagine having a puzzle and all the pieces are in a box without the cover. If I dumped all the pieces out on the table, picked up a piece, and told you that I could see where it fits in the puzzle, I would be deceiving you. You should certainly have doubts concerning my ability to see the picture clearly.

But if I put the whole puzzle together except for one piece, I could show you where the piece fits and how it completes the overall picture. If you looked at the nearly completed puzzle as I explained the picture, you could easily see where that piece fits and how it relates to the whole picture. Then you could draw your own conclusions.

Topical preaching has its place in the church, but if you don't see the whole picture of the Bible, all you absorb are bits and pieces that are hard to relate to. I believe knowledge comes by the Holy Spirit through voluminous reading. Read the Bible, not simply to memorize it, but to read it cover to cover like any book. Soon you will get the whole picture. You will see how the characters fit into the stories and how the stories make up the whole body of knowledge.

Studying the characters individually does not always provide the information you need to link them together, either. It's as if you had a great mystery novel and only read the last chapter. Yes, you know who-did-it, but you never come to grasp the whole of their life, who they were, what led them to do what they did.

When you read the Bible as a book, you will become familiar with the characters. For example, if you open the Bible and begin to read about Thamar (Tamar) in Matthew 1:30 you can say, "Oh yes, I know Thamar from Genesis 38:1–19. Her husband died and his brother would not marry her and give her a child. She tricked Judah into sleeping with her so that she could have a child." The text will be well known to you and easy to recall. This is valuable not only for your edification, but knowing the scriptures helps when you find yourself in situations where someone needs words of wisdom. The scriptures will become relevant and beneficial to meet the need at hand.

Three Sets of Fourteen C D

As I read the scripture seeking a clearer understanding of the three sets of fourteen generations, I came to the law of the Kinsman Redeemer in Leviticus 25:8–25. You see, in The Law of Moses, God provided for his people by insuring that their property inheritance would remain in their own family and never be lost.

This is the way it worked. At the end of every 49 years, all personal debt an individual owed, whether for themselves or their lands, was redeemable if the debtor had the ability to repay the debt owed. However, if the debtor was unable to redeem (pay back) those debts or buy back his land, God's Law stated that a close relative (near kinsman) could do so for him. In fact, if the relative had been born into or sold himself into slavery, the near kinsman could also buy that relative back out of slavery.

"And thou shalt number seven sabbaths of years unto thee, seven times seven years; and the space of the seven sabbaths of years shall be unto thee forty and nine years. Then shalt thou cause the trumpet of the jubile to sound on the tenth day of the seventh month, in the day of atonement shall ye make the trumpet sound throughout all your land. And ye shall hallow the fiftieth year, and proclaim liberty throughout all the land unto all the inhabitants thereof: it shall be a jubile unto you; and ye shall return every man unto his possession, and ye shall return every man unto his family. A jubile shall that fiftieth year be unto you: ye shall not sow, neither reap that which groweth of itself in it, nor gather the grapes in it of thy vine undressed. For it is the jubile; it shall be holy unto you: ye shall eat the increase thereof out of the field. In the year of this jubile ye shall return every man unto his possession. And if thou sell ought unto thy neighbour, or buyest ought of thy neighbour's hand, ye shall not oppress one another: According to the number of years after the jubile thou shalt buy of thy neighbour, and according unto the number of years of the fruits he shall sell unto thee: According to the multitude of years thou shalt increase the price thereof, and according to the fewness of years thou shalt diminish the price of it: for according to the number of the years of the fruits doth he sell unto thee. Ye shall not therefore oppress one another; but thou shalt fear thy God: for I am the LORD your God. Wherefore ye shall do my statutes, and keep my judgments, and do them; and ye shall dwell in the land in safety. And the land shall yield her fruit, and ye shall eat your fill, and dwell therein in safety. And if ye shall say, What shall we eat the seventh year? behold, we shall not sow, nor gather in our increase: Then I will command my blessing upon you in the sixth year, and it shall bring forth fruit for three years. And ye shall sow the eighth year, and eat yet of old fruit until the ninth year; until her fruits come in ye shall eat of the old store. The land shall not be sold for ever: for the land is mine; for ye are strangers and sojourners with me. And in all the land of your possession ye shall grant a redemption for the land. If thy brother be waxen poor, and hath sold away some of his possession, and if any of his kin come to redeem it, then shall he redeem that which his brother sold."—*Leviticus 25:8-25*

Remember, all scripture testifies of Jesus Christ. He is mysteriously hidden in the Old Testament and revealed in the New Testament. As I read the Old Testament, I constantly look for Jesus. Here he is clearly seen as the Kinsman Redeemer who comes in the forty-ninth year to *redeem* that which was lost. A D

Before we discuss this Kinsman Redeemer, let's establish a few important facts about the word *redemption* and what it means to us. In the Old Testament, *Redemption* means to get your rights back and or to gain back a lost relationship. In the New Testament, redemption means the act of being ransomed (purchased) in full.

We are the purchased possession, redeemed by His blood

The price paid for our redemption was the blood of Jesus Christ, God's Word made flesh. Satan can't buy us back, for he has nothing as valuable as the blood of Jesus.

"Take heed therefore unto yourselves, and to all the flock, over the which the Holy Ghost hath made you overseers, to feed *the church* of God, which he hath *purchased with his own blood*." —*Acts 20:28* E

We are purchased and also sealed, waiting for redemption

The New Testament teaches that at the moment of salvation we are sealed, waiting for redemption. The word *sealed* implies that the believer is marked or stamped by the Holy Spirit for a determined purpose. The Holy Spirit is the *earnest*—the down payment or guarantee that we will be redeemed in the future. This is clearly stated in Ephesians.

"In whom ye also trusted, after that ye heard the word of truth, the gospel of your salvation: in whom also after that ye believed, *ye were sealed* with that holy Spirit of promise, Which is the earnest of our inheritance until *the redemption of the purchased possession,* unto the praise of his glory."—*Ephesians 1:13-14* E

Day of Redemption

In Leviticus 25, we find that on the forty-ninth day of atonement, in the fifty-year cycle (Jubile), the Kinsman Redeemer shows up to redeem. According to Jesus, this redeemer is a testimony of Himself, and we know from the New Testament that Jesus is our Redeemer. D S T

"For the Son of man is come to seek and to save that which was lost."—*Luke 19:10*

Therefore, when the Kinsman Redeemer came in the forty-ninth year on the Day of Atonement, he was foreshadowing the Lord Jesus coming on a forty-ninth something in the future to redeem Adam's race. Again, we are sure from scripture that Jesus came to be the sacrifice for the sins of Adam's race, "to give His life a ransom for many" (Matthew 20:28), in the forty-second generation from the promise of redemption given to Abraham (Matthew 1:17). B D E Z

The believer is sealed and waiting for redemption. *Waiting for redemption* simply means that the believer is waiting to be present with Jesus in eternity. This will happen either through our being absent from this body and present with the Lord (physical death), or at the time of the redemption of the church when living believers will be caught up to meet Him in the air and join those who have already gone to be with the Lord. S

As we await the day when we will be redeemed and be with the Lord, we can sing, "I've been redeemed," but we are not there yet. There is yet a future Day of Redemption. We are saved, sealed, and waiting for redemption. Remember, there is a Day of Redemption and a Day of Judgment spoken of in the New Testament.

"And grieve not the holy Spirit of God, whereby ye are sealed unto the *day of redemption*." —*Ephesians 4:30* D W

"Because he hath appointed *a day, in the which he will judge* the world in righteousness by that man whom he hath ordained..."—*Acts 17:31* S

One more seven-sevens time period

But there's more. In the Old and New Testaments the day of Passover falls on the fourteenth day of the first month. The Day of Atonement falls on the tenth day of the seventh month. Counting the first month as one and the seventh month as seven, we find that God placed Passover seven months before Atonement.

If we look at the Passover as Jesus being crucified on the cross (paying the price for the sins of the world and ransoming or purchasing mankind from slavery to sin and its master Satan), and Atonement as the Day of Redemption of the church, we see a gap of seven time periods between the cross and redemption. If we understand this to mean seven generations and add it to the forty-two generations of Matthew 1, we have a total of 49 generations. The Lord was crucified in the forty-second generation. Therefore, it will be another seven generations to reach the forty-ninth generation and the coming of the Redeemer and the Day of Redemption. D L W Z

The Church Age

Another interesting set of facts is found in the teachings of Jesus. First, He stated that the Word of God is the seed (Luke 8:11) which is sown in men's hearts causing them to become *the children of the kingdom*. The seed (Word of God) produces the crop (fruit), which grows until harvest time (Matthew 13:24–30; 38–43). L

Secondly, the Bible teaches that after Jesus arose, He went to sit at the Father's right hand until His enemies are put under His feet (1 Corinthians 15:25).

Third, in the parable of the tares, He sent his disciples into the world, the field (Matthew 13:38). This parable illustrates that the enemy will sow tares into the crop, but the Lord's angels will fix this when the harvest comes. In the meantime, however, the crop must grow to *its fullness* (Romans 11:25) before the harvest, at which time the wheat and tares will be separated.

In the Law of Moses the same pattern is demonstrated when we look from Passover to Atonement. Passover is in the spring or planting time, and Atonement is placed by God at the time of harvest. In between are the seven months of growth for the crop. As I see it, the church age is typed or shadowed by the growing period between the Passover and the Atonement. Something has to be planted in order to have a harvest.

With this foundation regarding our Redemption, let's continue exploring the Kinsman Redeemer in Leviticus.

"Then shalt thou cause the trumpet of the jubile to sound on the tenth day of the seventh month, *in the day of atonement shall ye make the trumpet sound throughout all your land.* And ye shall hallow the fiftieth year, and proclaim liberty throughout all the land unto all the inhabitants thereof: it shall be a jubile unto you; and ye shall return every man unto his possession, and ye shall return every man unto his family."—*Leviticus 25:9, 10*

Notice that there is a trumpet which connects the Kinsman Redeemer and the Day of Atonement. The only time that the trumpet will blow on the Day of Atonement is in the forty-ninth year!

Therefore I conclude that this trumpet of Jubile is a figure of the trumpet that will be blown at the end of the forty-ninth generation. It signifies the Day of Redemption of the purchased possession by the Lamb, the true Kinsman Redeemer. The manifestation of the trumpet blowing is in 1 Thessalonians. D W

"...the Lord himself shall descend from heaven with a shout, with the voice of the archangel, and *with the trump of God...*"
—*1 Thessalonians 4:16*

The trumpet of Jubile spoken of in Leviticus foreshadows the "talking" trumpet spoken of in Revelation.

"...and the first voice which I heard was as it were *of a trumpet* talking with me; which said, Come up hither..."—*Revelation 4:1*

In Revelation 5:6 we see the *lamb slain.* In the law of Moses there was a lamb slain at Passover (the time of planting) which delivered the people from death yet they had to wait for their Atonement (the harvest) to take place.

At Passover, Jesus paid for our redemption. He was the seed planted in John 12:24. Z

Verily, verily, I say unto you, Except a corn of wheat fall into the ground and die, it abideth alone: but if it die, it bringeth forth much fruit.
—*John 12:24*

Yet, believers are still waiting for their redemption. When Jesus comes into the throne room as the *lamb slain*, we see the purchaser and the price He paid. W

As He comes into the throne room the purchased sing a song that only they can sing.

"...for thou wast slain, and *hast redeemed us* to God by thy blood out of every kindred, and tongue, and people, and nation; And hast made us unto our God kings and priests: and we shall reign on the earth."—*Revelation 5: 9,10* S

Review

There is a seven generation time period, or *seven times*, between the forty-second generation (the Passover Lamb) and the forty-ninth generation (the Kinsman Redeemer).

"And thou shalt number seven sabbaths of years unto thee, seven times seven years; and the space of the seven sabbaths of years shall be unto thee forty and nine years. Then shalt thou cause the trumpet of the jubile to sound on the tenth day of the seventh month, in the day of atonement..."—*Leviticus 25:8, 9*

So there are seven, seven-year Sabbaths ending at the number 49 which ushers in the Year of Jubile. The Year of Jubile is where everything that had been lost is returned to the rightful owners. T

Wait—there's more! After the Kinsman redeemed, and before the people could rightfully take full possession of that which was redeemed, there was another feast that began the year of Jubile, the Feast of Tabernacles. All who had been affected by the redeemer were told to move from their redeemed possessions and move into tents separating themselves from the world for seven days.

Each morning they were to wave branches unto the Lord and thank Him for the completed harvest (Leviticus 23:40–42). From my viewpoint, this shadows the seven years of the church celebrating the harvest of the earth in the heavens with the Redeemer. In Revelation 7:9,10 a multitude in white robes are waving palm branches before the Lord and celebrating their salvation.

In his first chapter, Matthew states that Jesus was born in the forty-second generation. I believe that six of the seven (seven Sabbaths) as presented in Leviticus, foreshadow these forty-two generations. The seven remaining generations foreshadow the church resting in the finished work of God (Hebrews 4:9–11). God isn't interested in returning earthly possessions to people, nor is He going about setting up a perfect form of earthly government before he comes. He is testifying of Jesus Christ. S L Z

I believe the blowing of the trumpet in the forty-ninth year on the Day of Atonement foreshadows the day when the Lord and the redeemed will come with all that have gone to rest in Him, and the living believers will be taken into heaven and all be with the Lord forever. Consider again this verse in Leviticus. D

"If thy brother be waxen poor, and hath sold away some of his possession [if he can't redeem himself], and if any of his kin come to redeem it, then shall he redeem that which his brother sold."—*Leviticus 25:25*

This world's god

The earth and all the things therein have been lost to Satan. In 2 Corinthians 4:4 the Bible says that Satan is the god of this world. The Bible also teaches that when Adam and Eve gave themselves over to Satan in the garden, they lost everything. They entered into death and therefore had to be redeemed. They could not redeem themselves. They tried to cover their nakedness (shame) with fig leaves, but their own works (leaves) withered, still ashamed, God covered them with animal skins (Genesis 3:7, 21) to cover their sin.

The *Kinsman Redeemer* is Jesus Christ. The scripture states that He is *our brother.*

"Saying, I will declare thy name unto my *brethren*, in the midst of the church will I sing praise unto thee."—*Hebrews 2:12*

Hebrews also declares:

"Forasmuch then as the children are partakers of flesh and blood, he also himself likewise took part of the same; that through death he might destroy him that had the power of death, that is, the devil; And deliver them who through fear of death were all their lifetime subject to bondage."—*Hebrews 2:14, 15* A E

Jesus came to *redeem* us from death. He became our kin, with flesh and blood like us, making him our *Kinsman Redeemer.* D

Our Redeemer is coming

The Kinsman Redeemer came to redeem in the forty-ninth year. Jesus was born in the forty-second generation to become the Passover Lamb. Therefore in the forty-ninth generation, Jesus will return as the *Kinsman Redeemer.* A E D

In the first three chapters of Revelation, there are seven letters written to the seven churches. The letters represent the chronological history of the church foretold by Jesus to John the apostle. The letter of the Church of Ephesus represents the forty-third generation and the letter of the Laodicean church represents the forty-ninth generation, which we live in. L

The Final Generation L

You may ask, "How do you know we are in the forty-ninth generation?" Jesus gives the answer in Luke. O

"And they shall fall by the edge of the sword, and shall be led away captive into all nations: and Jerusalem shall be trodden down of the Gentiles, until the times of the Gentiles be fulfilled."—*Luke 21:24*

"Verily I say unto you, This *generation* shall not pass away, till all be fulfilled."—*Luke 21:32*

The book of Matthew starts out by referring to generations. When Jesus spoke of Israel being reestablished as a nation (which took place on May 14, 1948), and this event signaling the final generation, He was establishing the fulfillment of the 49 generations. God never stops anything at forty-two. He never finishes at six sevens, He always finishes at seven sevens. Seven seals, seven years, etc. D

Summary

I believe that the remaining seventh generation between His first and Second Coming is depicted as the seven Gentile church ages shown through letters to the seven churches in Revelation chapters 1–3.

At the end of the letters to the seven churches in Revelation the scripture speaks of a *trumpet.*

"...and the first voice which I heard was as it were of a trumpet talking with me; which said, Come up hither, and I will shew thee things which must be hereafter. And immediately I was in the spirit: and, behold, a throne was set in heaven, and one sat on the throne." —*Revelation 4:1, 2*

John is taken up into heaven immediately. I believe this depicts the *catching away of the church.* We are told to watch and listen for the trumpet to blow. We have read in the scriptures that Jesus would come with a shout and the voice of an archangel and the trumpet of God for His church. W

And when these things begin to come to pass, then look up, and lift up your heads; for your redemption draweth nigh...Verily I say unto you, This generation shall not pass away, till all be fulfilled."—*Luke 21:28, 32*

Chapter 4: The Result of Sin

The carrying away of the Children of Israel into Babylon in the twenty-eighth generation was such a monumental event that God mentions it when He writes about the birth of Christ in Matthew 1:17.

We need to ask ourselves, "What happened that caused God to place such importance on this event? Why were the people carried away to Babylon? What did the people do that caused God to judge them in this way, allowing the Babylonians to take them into captivity?" God does not use empty words when he testifies of Jesus Christ.

The section of scripture concerning the *carrying away into Babylon* is found in 2 Kings 24:1–3. Remember, we must look at the whole story. A puzzle will not come together if you only view a few pieces. Scripture needs to be studied as a *whole.* A novel is incomplete with only a beginning or ending. F

"And the LORD sent against him bands of the Chaldees, and bands of the Syrians, and bands of the Moabites, and bands of the children of Ammon, and sent them against Judah to destroy it, according to the word of the LORD, which he spake by his servants the prophets. Surely at the commandment of the LORD came this upon Judah, to remove them out of his sight, for the *sins of Manasseh*, according to all that he did."—*2 Kings 24:2, 3* G

As Judah is carried away into Babylon (verses 2–3), we see in verse 7 that Judah is being removed from the promised land.

"...for the king of Babylon had taken from the river of Egypt unto the river Euphrates all that pertained to the king of Egypt."—*2 Kings 24:7*

The land from the river of Egypt to the Euphrates River is the boundary of the land which God had given to Abraham.

"In the same day the LORD made a covenant with Abram, saying, Unto thy seed have I given this land, from the river of Egypt unto the great river, the river Euphrates."—*Genesis 15:18*

So God removed the Children of Israel from land promised to Abraham, and delivered them into the hands of the Babylonians. Why? Because of the *sins of Manasseh* (2 Kings 24:3). The details of Manasseh's deeds will be covered in *Chapter 5: Cause of Remaining Judgment.* G

What is sin?

Sin is identified in many ways in scripture. The actual meaning for sin in the Bible is *missing the mark*. Biblically, the end result of sin is *bondage*. If a person refuses to repent of sin, they place themselves in danger of being taken captive by the consequences of sin. But, because of the blood of Jesus Christ and His finished work on the cross, God seeks to deliver you from sin.

Just as it was futile for Adam and Eve to attempt to cover their sin with fig leaves, so it is impossible for you to use your own works to cover your own sin. It makes no difference what kind of good works you use attempting to merit God's grace—it's not enough. God removes our sin based solely on the shed blood offered by His Son Jesus Christ, the perfect sacrifice substituted in our place. To take advantage of His sacrifice for your sin, you must accept Him by faith alone.

Plan of restoration

Now with the stage set, and with Israel in captivity in Babylon, let's look at the plan of restoration God has for His people and the Promised Land.

The time line

In the Old Testament book of Daniel, we find a Jewish man of God named Daniel who had been taken captive as a boy (2 Kings 24:1–3). As he grew to manhood, God greatly used him as a prophet, and elevated him to a high position in the government of Babylon. Daniel was a student of the scripture scrolls available in his day. This same scripture from Jeremiah can still be read in our day. F I

"In the first year of Darius the son of Ahasuerus, of the seed of the Medes, which was made king over the realm of the Chaldeans; In the first year of his reign *I Daniel understood by books the number of the years*, whereof the word of the LORD came to Jeremiah the prophet, that he would accomplish seventy years in the desolations of Jerusalem."—*Daniel 9:1, 2*

God had told Jeremiah that Israel would be carried away to Babylon and that they would be released at the end of seventy years. Daniel read the book of Jeremiah, and understanding the times[†] that he was living in, Daniel concluded, that the prophesied seventy years of captivity were completed. This realization caused Daniel to set his face to seek the Lord.

"For thus saith the LORD, That after seventy years be accomplished at Babylon I will visit you, and perform my good word toward you, in causing you to return to this place."
—*Jeremiah 29:10*

"And this whole land shall be a desolation, and an astonishment; and these nations shall serve the king of Babylon seventy years. And it shall come to pass, when seventy years are accomplished, that I will punish the king of Babylon, and that nation, saith the LORD, for their iniquity, and the land of the Chaldeans, and will make it perpetual desolations."
—*Jeremiah 25:11–12*

That line today

In our day and age, we too are faced with scripture that calls for action.

"And they shall fall by the edge of the sword, and shall be led away captive into all nations: and Jerusalem shall be trodden down of the Gentiles, *until the times of the Gentiles be fulfilled.*"—Luke 21:24

[†]Roger Oakland's site: www.understandthetimes.org

In Luke 21:24 we are told that the Jews would be taken captive and dispersed among the nations a second time. At the end of this captivity, the Jews would again return to their land and Jerusalem would belong to them. O

In 1948 Israel became a nation and in 1967 Israel took Jerusalem. Can we be like Daniel? Daniel read and believed the Word of God. He easily figured out that the seventy years of Babylonian captivity were nearing completion. He knew he was living in the generation in which God would free His people. We, too, have a sign in our day. I O

And when these things begin to come to pass, then look up, and lift up your heads; for your redemption draweth nigh…Verily I say unto you, *This generation* shall not pass away, till *all be fulfilled."—Luke 21:28, 32*

Remember, I believe *this generation*, the *last generation*, and the *forty-ninth generation*, are one and the same. I do know that all will be fulfilled in the generation that sees Israel reestablished (Luke 21:24). D

As Daniel acted in his generation, we too should act in this generation.

"And I set my face unto the Lord God, to seek by prayer and supplications, with fasting, and sackcloth, and ashes."—*Daniel 9:3*

Daniel knew what God was going to do. Therefore, he set his face to seek the Lord.

"And I prayed unto the LORD my God, and made my confession, and said, O Lord, the great and dreadful God, keeping the covenant and mercy to them that love him, and to them that keep his commandments; *We have sinned, and have committed iniquity,* and have done wickedly, and have rebelled, even by departing from thy precepts and from thy judgments."
—Daniel 9:4, 5

Confession before God

Daniel confessed his sins and his nation's sins. The truth and the awareness of the sins of this current day should provoke one to repent and seek the Lord.

I was aware that scripture was fulfilled when Israel became a nation in 1948. So when Jerusalem became part of Israel on June 8, 1967, I realized I was witnessing the fulfillment of Luke 21:24. I went to my knees and began fasting and praying. O

"And it shall come to pass in that day, that the Lord shall set his hand again the second time to recover the remnant of his people, which shall be left, from Assyria, and from Egypt, and from Pathros, and from Cush, and from Elam, and from Shinar, and from Hamath, and from the islands of the sea. And he shall set up an ensign for the nations, and shall assemble the outcasts of Israel, and gather together the dispersed of Judah from the four corners of the earth."—*Isaiah 11:11–12*

This new fulfillment of scripture ignited a new zeal in my heart. As I set my face towards God, I petitioned Him for direction. Excitedly I prayed, "This is really happening! What should I do?" This scripture in 2 Peter took on new meaning.

"Seeing then that all these things shall be dissolved, what manner of persons ought ye to be in all holy *conversation* and *godliness."*
—2 Peter 3:11

Lifestyle changes

In this verse the word *conversation* means *manner of life*. I pondered, what should I be like in my *manner of life*? The word *godliness* means *devotion to God*. What should I be like in my *devotion*? Peter was posing the question directly to me, "What kind of person should I be, if everything written in the scriptures is true?"

That's really a question for all of us. If this is the last generation and the Bible testifies that Jesus Christ is coming back, "What kind of people should we be?"

Should we be frivolous pleasure seekers claiming our right to worldly possessions, or should we be really devoted to God with our faces toward Him, seeking Him to show us how we can best be used? D

Refocus

I believe God gives us this knowledge to keep Jesus Christ as the central focus of our lives and His soon return as the motivation for daily living. As I set my face toward the Lord, seeking Him in prayer, He called me to go to the streets. I spent ten years in that ministry, most of it with a beard and long hair, something I had never done before in my life. I went in this disguise among hippies leading them to Christ through the words that the Lord gave me day by day. Tens of thousands of young people gave their lives to the Lord through the ministry that He had ordained. I feel that the Lord used me in this way because I set my face toward God and said, "Lord, look at this day that we live in. What should I do?"

Daniel's question

Daniel was more than eighty years old when he asked, "What should I do?" As he confessed his sins, he reaffirmed that God was righteous in that He had judged Israel because they had sinned against God. I

"Neither have we obeyed the voice of the LORD our God, to walk in his laws, which he set before us by his servants the prophets. Yea, all Israel have transgressed thy law, even by departing, that they might not obey thy voice; therefore the *curse* is poured upon us, and the oath that is written in the law of Moses the servant of God, because we have sinned against him."
—Daniel 9:10,11

Daniel's conclusion

Daniel is essentially saying, "I know what age and generation I live in, and I've seen that we've sinned and are therefore under the curse."

Upon reading this verse I immediately asked myself, "What curse? Where in the law is there a curse? When did God curse Israel?" After searching, I found several places that contain a curse. We will cover the one in Leviticus chapter 26.

The Commandments and the Curse

In chapter 26 of Leviticus, God tells the nation of Israel to keep two of the commandments He had already given them in Exodus 20.

"*Ye shall make you no idols nor graven image*, neither rear you up a standing image, neither shall ye set up any image of stone in your land, to bow down unto it: for I am the LORD your God. *Ye shall keep my sabbath*s, and reverence my sanctuary: I am the LORD."
—Leviticus 26:1, 2 I J

Here God is stressing two particular commandments: the second commandment dealing with idolatry, and the fourth commandment about keeping the Sabbath. There is blessing for them if they keep these commandments, and a consequence (curse) if they do not (Leviticus 26:14–39).

This is an interesting place for a curse because in Leviticus chapter 25, God promised Israel a Redeemer.

"But if ye will not hearken unto me, and will not do all these commandments; And if ye shall despise my statutes, or if your soul abhor my judgments, so that ye will not do all my commandments, but that ye break my covenant: I also will do this unto you; I will even appoint over you terror, consumption, and the burning ague, that shall consume the eyes, and cause sorrow of heart: and ye shall sow your seed in vain, for your enemies shall eat it. And I will set my face against you, and ye shall be slain before your enemies: they that hate you shall reign over you; and ye shall flee when none pursueth you. And if ye will not yet for all this hearken unto me, then I will punish you *seven times* more for your sins."
—Leviticus 26:14–18 I

The Curse for breaking the Second Commandment

The Second Commandment has to do with worshipping the true God, and not idols.

"Thou shalt not make unto thee any graven image, or any likeness of any thing that is in heaven above, or that is in the earth beneath, or that is in the water under the earth: Thou shalt not bow down thyself to them, nor serve them: for I the LORD thy God am a jealous God, visiting the iniquity of the fathers upon the children unto the third and fourth generation of them that hate me; And shewing mercy unto thousands of them that love me, and keep my commandments."*—Exodus 20:4–6*

God promised a punishment upon those who made images or statues and worshipped them. All of God's commandments have deep meanings and far reaching consequences, but this is the only commandment which directly contains a consequence (a curse) for disobeying it.

Another book? Not again!

I grew up in a church that had a different way to deal with God's commandments. This church had a book other than the Word of God. They did use the Bible, but in my day no one was allowed to read it except the ordained. In their book on page 496, which is presently called *The Catechism of the Catholic Church*, three views of the Ten Commandments are shown.

The traditional catechismal formula includes the Ten Commandments that I learned as a child in the church school. You will notice that the second commandment has been changed from its original state.

"Thou shalt not make unto thee any graven image, or any likeness of any thing that is in heaven above, or that is in the earth beneath, or that is in the water under the earth: Thou shalt not bow down thyself to them, nor serve them…"*—Exodus 20:4, 5*

To *read:* "You shall not take the name of the Lord God in vain."

In those days that church simply removed the second commandment and split the tenth, making it into two. They then moved all the commandments up to replace the second with the third, and so on. Of course, that particular church has graven images all over the place.

Now, in their new Catechism they combine the true first and second commandments into one, still splitting the tenth, and moving them all up. However, now they address the subject of graven images in a very interesting way.

If you look on pages 516 and 517 of *The Catechism of the Catholic Church*, you'll find some futile attempts to explain away graven images. I quote directly from this book.

Article 1, Part IV: *The First Commandment—You shall not make for yourself a graven image."*

No. 2131: "Basing itself on the mystery of the incarnate word, the seventh ecumenical council at Nicaea (787) justified against the iconoclasts the veneration of icons—of Christ, but also the Mother of God, the angels, and all the saints. By becoming incarnate, the Son of God introduced a new 'economy.' "

No. 2132: "The Christian veneration of images is not contrary to the first commandment which proscribes idols. Indeed, 'the honor rendered to an image passes to its prototype,' and 'whoever venerates an image venerates the person portrayed in it.' The honor paid to sacred images is a 'respectful veneration,' not the adoration due to God alone."

That is a convenient way to explain away sin, but in the New Testament Apostle John also warns against idols.

"Little children, keep yourselves from idols. Amen."—*1 John 5:21*

Enter Jezebel

Jesus Himself warned the Thyatira church (generation) concerning the woman Jezebel who would try to seduce the servants of God.

"Notwithstanding I have a few things against thee, because thou sufferest that woman Jezebel, which calleth herself a prophetess, to teach and to seduce my servants to commit fornication, and to eat things sacrificed unto idols. And I gave her space to repent of her fornication; and she repented not. Behold, I will cast her into a bed, and them that commit adultery with her into great tribulation, except they repent of their deeds. And I will kill her children with death; and all the churches shall know that I am he which searcheth the reins and hearts: and I will give unto every one of you according to your works. But unto you I say, and unto the rest in Thyatira, as many as have not this doctrine, and which have not known the depths of Satan, as they speak; I will put upon you none other burden."—*Revelation 2:20–24*

If you study the Old Testament you will find that Jezebel was the wife of wicked King Ahab. She was also a Zidonian, and introduced the idolatrous worship of Baal and Ashtaroth into the northern kingdom of Israel. The Zidonian people were known for their worship of the false goddess Ashtaroth, known as the *Queen of Heaven*.

Idolatrous worship was first introduced to Israel under King Solomon and led directly to the nation splitting into two nations. Eventually these idolatrous practices found their way into the southern kingdom of Judah and contributed to the *sins of Manasseh*. Judah adopted idolatry while continuing their worship of the true God through the Temple ceremonies. G

Judah had several good kings that led revivals, which held back the nation's march towards reprobation through the worship of false gods and idolatry. However, the northern kingdom lacked Godly kings and slid steadily into reprobation through this satanic practice.

In 722 B.C. the northern kingdom fell under the curse of Leviticus 26, and went into captivity in Assyria and eventually was scattered among the nations until 1948. The southern kingdom had one last revival under King Josiah, but within 130 years of its sister nation's desertion of God, Judah came under the curse, and was taken into Bablylon in 586 B.C. This is the history that the prophet Daniel read in the book of Jeremiah. I Z

Spiritual wickedness

When Jesus warned the churches of Jezebel, He knew she was dead, but He was warning of the spiritual wickedness of the idolatry that she introduced. Jesus, referring to this wickedness, calls it the *depths of Satan* (Revelation 2:24).

I can only conclude that the worship of *icons* is Satanic. Whether you call the object an icon or an idol they are the same wicked, satanic, evil influence in the body of Christ. The believer needs to stay clear of idols (1 John 5:21), and not allow their use to be rationalized.

The Curse for breaking the Sabbath

Now let's examine the second part of the cause of the curse. It is centered around the consequence of failing to keep the Sabbath.

In Leviticus, the Lord gives a clear commandment to Israel concerning the land and its rest (Sabbath).

"Speak unto the children of Israel, and say unto them, When ye come into the land which I give you, *then shall the land keep a sabbath* unto the LORD. Six years thou shalt sow thy field, and six years thou shalt prune thy vineyard, and gather in the fruit thereof; But in the seventh year shall be a *sabbath of rest* unto the land, *a sabbath* for the LORD: thou shalt neither sow thy field, nor prune thy vineyard. That which groweth of its own accord of thy harvest thou shalt not reap, neither gather the grapes of thy vine undressed: for it is *a year of rest unto the land.*" *—Leviticus 25:2–5*

If the Jews did not keep the Sabbath and did not allow the land its Sabbaths, God said He would remove them from the land so the land could get its Sabbath rests. F I J N X

'And *I will scatter you among the heathen*, and will draw out a sword after you: and your land shall be desolate, and your cities waste. *Then shall the land enjoy her sabbaths*, as long as it lieth desolate, and ye be in your enemies' land; even then shall the land rest, and enjoy her sabbaths."*—Leviticus 26:33, 34*

"To fulfil the word of the LORD by the mouth of Jeremiah, *until the land had enjoyed her sabbaths:* for as long as she lay desolate she kept sabbath, to fulfil *threescore and ten years."—2 Chronicles 36:21*

Seventy Sabbaths

Here we can see the reason for the seventy years of captivity in Babylon. About the time Saul was anointed king by Samuel, Israel stopped keeping the Sabbath rests (1095 B.C.), 490 years before the Babylonian Captivity. Mathematically, if you divide seven into 490, this results in seventy Sabbaths not kept. Therefore, God put them in captivity for seventy years, which allowed the land to rest, and fulfilled His promise to the land. I X

Back to Leviticus 26 and the curse

In Leviticus 26 God promises *seven periods of judgment* upon His people if they disobeyed his commandments. When they refused to repent, He repeated this seven period judgment three more times. Four times seven equals *twenty-eight*. This is the period of judgment when the people of Israel were carried away into Babylon—the twenty-eighth generation (Leviticus 26:33). I

Judgment upon Israel came in four parts. It is interesting that both the carrying away to Babylon and the end of the four periods of judgment both came about on the twenty-eighth generation. F

On a positive note, God tells the people that if they would only confess their iniquity and the iniquities of their fathers, then He would remember his convenant. K

"If they shall confess their iniquity, and the iniquity of their fathers, with their trespass which they trespassed against me, and that also they have walked contrary unto me; And that I also have walked contrary unto them, and have brought them into the land of their enemies; if then their uncircumcised hearts be humbled, and they then accept of the punishment of their iniquity: Then will I remember my covenant with Jacob, and also my covenant with Isaac, and also my covenant with Abraham will I remember; and I will remember the land."—*Leviticus 26:40–42*

Do you recall what God's covenant with Abraham said? It said that God would send His *seed*, Jesus Christ, and all the nations would be *blessed by His seed.* B

"And in *thy seed* shall all the nations of the earth be blessed; because thou hast obeyed my voice."—*Genesis 22:18*

"Now to Abraham and *his seed* were the promises made. He saith not, And to seeds, as of many; but as of one, And to *thy seed, which is Christ."—Galations 3:16*

The consummation of the promise was and is Jesus Christ. Even as Israel faced judgment for their sins, God remembered His promise to Abraham. B E F I

Let's now conclude this chapter by simply stating that the seventy years of captivity in Babylon paid for the violation of the Sabbath. We have yet to see the judgment for breaking the second commandment. The judgment for the *sins of Manasseh* will soon be pronounced!

"Thou, even thou, art to be feared: and who may stand in thy sight when once thou art angry? Thou didst cause judgment to be heard from heaven; the earth feared, and was still, When God arose to judgment, to save all the meek of the earth. Selah."—*Psalm 76:7–9*

Chapter 5: Cause of Remaining Judgment

The nation of Israel was forewarned by God in the law of Moses (Leviticus 26), as to what would happen if they did not keep the Second Commandment and the Sabbath rests, or if they refused His chastisement. The law stated that God's curse would come upon them and they would be scattered among the unbelieving nations.

Silence of Scriptures

This scattering is not mentioned again in the books of Joshua, Judges, Ruth, or First and Second Samuel. Throughout these books, Israel worshipped idols (including Baal and Ashtaroth), offered sacrifices in high places, and practiced the abominations of the peoples they had driven from the land. Despite these things, scattering was never mentioned by any of the judges or prophets of those times.

Forewarned again

When David came to power, the nation of Israel was united under one King. David's son Solomon assumed the throne of the united kingdom and was visited by God and given great wisdom. Through the direction of his father David and the inspiration of God's wisdom, King Solomon began to build the Temple of God in Jerusalem.

The Temple faced the Kidron Valley. Upon its completion, God again appeared to Solomon (1 Kings 9:1–9), and said that He would keep his promise to his father David, if Solomon walked in God's ways. However if Solomon turned from following God's ways and served other gods, God *warned* that He would cut Israel off from the land, *scatter them* among the heathen, and destroy the Temple. Y

At this point in history, the curse found in Leviticus chapter 26 is again mentioned by God. Therefore, I conclude that the desecration of the Temple and the invoking of the curse to be synonymous. G

The Ark and Solomon's wife

In 1 Kings 9:24 is an interesting detail that reveals the mentality of King Solomon. He married Pharaoh's daughter (an unscriptural marriage), and moved her out of the City of David to a house he had built for her. The reason for the move is found in 2 Chronicles.

"And Solomon brought up the daughter of Pharaoh out of the City of David unto the house that he had built for her: for he said, My wife shall not dwell in the house of David king of

Israel, *because the places are holy,* whereunto the ark of the LORD hath come."
—2 Chronicles 8:11

Solomon knew about holiness and he knew about uncleanliness. If the Ark of the Covenant made the City of David holy, then certainly its presence in the Holy of Holies made the Temple holy. So when the Temple was completed, Solomon moved the Ark of the Covenant out of the City of David, down through the Kidron Valley, and up to the Temple to its resting place in the Holy of Holies.

On tour

In March of 1995, I had the privilege of standing upon the ruins of the City of David in Israel. From this vantage point, I could see the Kidron Valley and the different entrances to the Temple Mount. In my mind's eye, I could picture the grandeur of David's City and the movement of God's Holy Ark as it was carried out of the city, down the Valley, and up onto the Temple Mount. I could also look to my right and see the point where the Hinnom Valley meets the Kidron Valley.

The Hinnom Valley's history came flooding into my mind. About 234 years after Solomon had built the Temple, Solomon's descendant, King Ahaz, the grandfather of Manasseh, began sacrificing his children in the Hinnom Valley. His heathenistic actions progressed to include defilement of the Temple. These evil actions begun by Ahaz would culminate in the total defilement of the city and the Holy Temple.

A deeper look at Ahaz

To give a bit of background, Ahaz is spoken of in 2 Kings chapter 16 and 2 Chronicles chapter 28. In 2 Kings 16, we find that Ahaz did not do that which was right in the sight of the Lord. He walked in the ways of the heathen and made his sons pass through the fire. He did according to the abominations of the heathen whom the Lord God cast out before the Children of Israel.

In 2 Chronicles 28:2, Ahaz made molten images for Baalim. Second Kings chapter 16 records that he was attacked by the King of northern Israel and the King of Syria. At the same time, 2 Chronicles states that many of the neighboring countries invaded Judah and caused havoc in the land. Many Judeans were carried away captive.

"For the LORD brought Judah low because of Ahaz king of Israel; for he made Judah naked, and transgressed sore against the LORD."
—2 Chronicles 28:19

Regrettably, Ahaz, because of this trouble, turned to King Tiglathpileser of Assyria, for help instead of seeking the Lord. Ahaz took silver and gold out of the Temple of God and gave it to King Tiglathpileser.

"For Ahaz took away a portion out of the house of the LORD, and out of the house of the king, and of the princes, and gave it unto the king of Assyria: but he helped him not."
—2 Chronicles 28:21

Ahaz hired King Tiglathpileser to defeat the king of Syria and drive back the Israelite army of the north. Afterwards, King Ahaz visited the defeated Syrians in the Syrian capital of Damascus. There he discovered an altar used to sacrifice to false gods. He then charged his priests to duplicate this altar in Jerusalem at the Temple.

Upon his return to Jerusalem, Ahaz had the people sacrifice burnt offerings, meat offerings, and drink offerings, sprinkling the blood of these sacrifices upon the false altar.

However, Ahaz offered his sacrifices at the true altar on the north side of the Temple.

Ahaz also cut off the legs and removed the oxen from under the laver (Sea of Brass) which was before the Temple, thus lowering the laver to the pavement.

"And in the time of his distress did he trespass yet more against the LORD: this is that king Ahaz. For he sacrificed unto the gods of Damascus, which smote him: and he said, Because the gods of the kings of Syria help them, therefore will I sacrifice to them, that they may help me. But they were the ruin of him, and of all Israel. And Ahaz gathered together the vessels of the house of God, and cut in pieces the vessels of the house of God, and shut up the doors of the house of the LORD, and he made him altars in every corner of Jerusalem. And in every several city of Judah he made high places to burn incense unto other gods, and provoked to anger the LORD God of his fathers."
—2 Chronicles 28:22–25

Ahaz verses Manasseh

Why didn't God scatter the people of Israel for the sins of Ahaz? The answer is in 2 Chronicles 28:24. Ahaz stopped in his desecration of the Temple by shutting it up and not defiling the Holy of Holies which his grandson Manasseh eventually would do. The abomination that caused the desolation of Jerusalem would be the placing of the idol in the Holy of Holies by Manasseh. G H

Why did God eventually scatter Judah for the sins of Manasseh?

What did Manasseh do? He put an idol in the Temple. He broke the second commandment—he replaced the Ark of the Covenant with the idol of Ashtaroth's grove. He also burned his children and sacrificed his babies to idols, thereby declaring Baal to be God. G

"Manasseh was twelve years old when he began to reign, and reigned fifty and five years in Jerusalem. And his mother's name was Hephzibah. And he did that which was evil in the sight of the LORD, after the abominations of the heathen, whom the LORD cast out before the children of Israel. For he built up again the high places which Hezekiah his father had destroyed; and he reared up *altars for Baal,* and made a grove, as did Ahab king of Israel; and worshipped all the host of heaven, and served them. And *he built altars in the house of the LORD*, of which the LORD said, In Jerusalem will I put my name. And he built altars for all the host of heaven *in the two courts of the house of the LORD*. And *he made his son pass through the fire*, and observed times, and used enchantments, and dealt with familiar spirits and wizards: he wrought much wickedness in the sight of the LORD, to provoke him to anger. **And he set a graven image of the grove that he had made in the house, of which the LORD said to David, and to Solomon his son, In this house, and in Jerusalem, which I have chosen out of all tribes of Israel, will I put my name for ever:** Neither will I make the feet of Israel move any more out of the land which I gave their fathers; only if they will observe to do according to all that I have commanded them, and according to all the law that my servant Moses commanded them. But they hearkened not: and *Manasseh seduced them to do more evil than did the nations whom the LORD destroyed before the children of Israel*. And the LORD spake by his servants the prophets, saying, Because Manasseh king of Judah hath done these abominations, and *hath done wickedly above all that the Amorites did*, which were before him, and hath *made Judah also to sin with his idols*: Therefore thus saith the LORD God of Israel, Behold, I am bringing such evil upon Jerusalem and Judah, that whosoever heareth of it, both his ears shall tingle. And I will stretch over Jerusalem the line of Samaria, and the plummet of the house of Ahab: and I will wipe Jerusalem as a man wipeth a dish, wiping it, and turning it upside down. *And I will forsake the remnant of mine inheritance, and deliver them into the hand of their enemies*; and they shall become a prey and a spoil to all their enemies; Because they have done that which was evil in my sight, and have provoked me to anger, since the day their fathers came forth out of Egypt, even unto this day. Moreover *Manasseh shed innocent blood very much*, till he had filled Jerusalem from one end to another; beside his sin wherewith he made Judah to sin, in doing that which was evil in the sight of the LORD. Now the rest of the acts of Manasseh, and all that he did, and his sin that he sinned, are they not written in the book of the chronicles of the kings of Judah?—*2 Kings 21:1-17*

Direct Defiance

God told Solomon that He would tear the Temple down and scatter Judah among the nations if they worshipped any other gods (1 Kings 9:6–9). Manasseh put an idol in the Temple, and God kept His word and ultimately tore the temple down and scattered Judah among the nations. G

Daniel hears from God

Chapter four mentions the prayer of Daniel the prophet when he understood from reading the book of Jeremiah that the seventy years of judgment on Judah would soon come to an end—the debt for breaking the Sabbaths had been paid. At that time, Daniel sought the Lord, confessed sins, fasted, and prayed. Daniel had been praying all day when Gabriel showed up and explained about the seventy weeks of judgment on Jerusalem for their transgressions—for *the sins of Manasseh*.

"Yea, whiles I was speaking in prayer, even the man Gabriel, whom I had seen in the vision at the beginning, being caused to fly swiftly, touched me about the time of the evening oblation."—*Daniel 9:21*

"And he informed me, and talked with me, and said, O Daniel, I am now come forth to give thee skill and understanding. At the beginning of thy supplications the commandment came forth, and I am come to shew thee; for thou art greatly beloved: therefore understand the matter, and consider the vision. Seventy weeks are determined upon thy people and upon thy holy city, to finish the transgression, and to make an end of sins, and to make reconciliation for iniquity, and to bring in everlasting righteousness, and to seal up the vision and prophecy, and to anoint the most Holy."
—*Daniel 9:22–24*

Each day for a year

Before we go on, it is important to establish the fact that when God dealt with judgment, He set a precedent for converting a day to a year. You can understand this by reading the following passages from Numbers and Ezekiel.

"After the number of the days in which ye searched the land, even forty days, *each day for a year,* shall ye bear your iniquities, even forty years, and ye shall know my breach of promise."
—*Numbers 14:34*

In Ezekiel, God told Ezekiel to lay down for three hundred ninety days, each day representing a year of judgment.

"Lie thou also upon thy left side, and lay the iniquity of the house of Israel upon it: according to the number of the days that thou shalt lie upon it thou shalt bear their iniquity.
For I have laid upon thee the years of their iniquity, according to the number of the days, three hundred and ninety days: so shalt thou bear the iniquity of the house of Israel. And when thou hast accomplished them, lie again on thy right side, and thou shalt bear the iniquity of the house of Judah forty days: *I have appointed thee each day for a year.*"
—Ezekiel 4:4–6

Accurate prophecy

What makes Daniel's prophecy so important, besides being the inspired Word of God, is that it accurately proclaims to the day when the Messiah would ride into Jerusalem.

In Daniel's prophecy, seventy weeks were determined upon His people and the Holy City. The 70 weeks equal 490 days (70 weeks × 7 days). Converting the days to years results in 490 years. J I

The Angel Gabriel said that the *Messiah would be cut off 69 weeks (483 years)* after the commandment went forth to restore and rebuild Jerusalem (Daniel 9:25, 26). That *decree was given by Artaxerxes in March, 445* B.C. (Nehemiah 2:1–6). To this date we add the 483 years which were prophesied and that brings us to April, A.D. 32, the month many believe that Jesus rode into Jerusalem. The final week, the last seven years known as the Great Tribulation period, or the time of Jacob's trouble (Jeremiah 30:7), is yet to be fulfilled. E J K N P Z

Seventy weeks equals the number 490 which is also the number of forgiveness. We understand this by reading Jesus' response to Peter's question.

"Lord, how oft shall my brother sin against me, and I forgive him? till seven times? Jesus saith unto him, I say not unto thee, Until seven times: but, Until seventy times seven."
—Matthew 18:21, 22

This means someone has 490 times to repent!

"Seventy weeks are determined upon thy people and upon thy holy city, to finish the transgression, and to make an end of sins, and to make reconciliation for iniquity, and to bring in everlasting righteousness..."*—Daniel 9:24* J

Think about this phrase, "upon thy people and upon thy holy city." This determination is against the people of Israel and Jerusalem, not the world. Why not against the Gentiles? They didn't commit the *sins of Manasseh.* Why did the Jews come into judgment? For the *sins of Manasseh!* G F

"In his days Nebuchadnezzar king of Babylon came up, and Jehoiakim became his servant three years: then he turned and rebelled against him. And the LORD sent against him bands of the Chaldees, and bands of the Syrians, and bands of the Moabites, and bands of the children of Ammon, and sent them against Judah to destroy it, according to the word of the LORD, which he spake by his servants the prophets. Surely at the commandment of the LORD came this upon Judah, to remove them out of his sight, for the *sins of Manasseh*, according to all that he did."*—2 Kings 24:1-3*

Back to the scattering

During the first seventy years of this judgment, God dealt with the children of Judah because they broke the Sabbaths (Leviticus 26). Now God is going to deal with the remaining issue, the breaking of the Second Commandment. The descendants of those who break this commandment would be punished to the third and fourth generation.

"Thou shalt not make unto thee any graven image, or any likeness of any thing that is in heaven above, or that is in the earth beneath, or that is in the water under the earth: Thou shalt not bow down thyself to them, nor serve them: for I the LORD thy God am a jealous God, visiting the iniquity of the fathers upon the children unto the third and fourth generation of them that hate me."—*Exodus 20: 4–5*

The 490 years determined on the city and the people to make reconciliation for iniquity, that the angel Gabriel declared to Daniel (Daniel 9:24), was punishment for the *sins of Manasseh* (the breaking of the Second Commandment). J

Manasseh foreshadows the Antichrist

When Judah returned from the Babylonian captivity, they built another Temple for the Messiah to enter. Over 400 years later, the Messiah did enter that Temple. After the Messiah cleansed the Temple by driving out the money changers, He was rejected. Jesus then foretold the destruction of the Temple (Matthew 24) which was accomplished in A.D. 70. Another Temple will not be built until the Antichrist comes. J F I M

In the future, according to the Bible, Israel is going to accept the false messiah, the Antichrist. At the same time, they are also going to build a third Temple. The scripture states that the false messiah will have a false prophet that will build an image of this false one and place it in the third Temple. Scripture also states that the false one will sit in this Temple and declare himself to be God. Isn't it ironic that the *sins of Manasseh* will be duplicated? Satan, through his false messiah, will be standing in direct defiance of God. G H

I believe that in the future the Antichrist will be involved in building the new Temple, and after three-and-a-half years he will place his statue in the Holy of Holies and declare himself to be God.

"When ye therefore shall see the abomination of desolation, spoken of by Daniel the prophet, stand in the holy place…"—*Matthew 24:15*

"Who opposeth and exalteth himself above all that is called God, or that is worshipped; so that he as God sitteth in the temple of God, shewing himself that he is God."—*2 Thessalonians 2:4*

The Antichrist will declare himself to be God in direct defiance to God's judgment and will draw his anointing and power from Satan (Revelation 13:4). This is the same spirit that is behind all false gods. N H

One of the false spirits, Beelzebub, is mentioned in three of the gospels. This satanic name is most likely an alteration of ba´al zebûl, meaning exalted Baal, and means *dung god*. Is this someone you would want to follow? All the world is, even though it isn't consciously aware of the fact.

Who is this judgment on, and why?

The answer is Israel—for breaking the Second Commandment (the *sins of Manasseh*). The church, comprised of Jewish and Gentile believers, has nothing to do with what Manasseh did. The believers in Jesus Christ will not be in the time of great tribulation, Jacob's Troubles, for that period of time deals with Israel and with the Gentile nations which have rejected Christ! F G R W

Israel Reconciled—Believers Delivered

Behind everything is the fact that God is going to reconcile Israel to Himself as He brings them to the saving knowledge of their Messiah. Let's stop here and review for a moment what we have covered so far and how this relates to the deliverance of the believer from God's judgment. In the book of Daniel, Gabriel prophesies to Daniel. W

"Know therefore and understand, that from the going forth of the commandment to restore and to build Jerusalem *unto the Messiah the Prince shall be seven weeks, and threescore and two weeks:* the street shall be built again, and the wall, even in troublous times. And after threescore and two weeks shall Messiah be cut off, but not for himself..."—*Daniel 9:25, 26*

Sixty-nine weeks (483 years) are accounted for, leaving seven years to be fulfilled. These seven years are years of judgment upon Israel to finish the prophecy given to Daniel. They are known as the time of Great Tribulation (Matthew 24:2) and Jacob's Trouble (Jeremiah 30:7). It's also called the *Tribulation Period*, a phrase coined by mankind. According to the scriptures, this isn't guesswork. It is a fact. These coming years of judgment have nothing to do with the believers that have come under the purchasing power of the blood of Jesus. N S

1A
10

"For, lo, I *begin* to bring evil on the city which is called by my name, and should ye be utterly unpunished? Ye shall not be unpunished: for I will call for a sword upon all the inhabitants of the earth, saith the LORD of hosts."—*Jeremiah 25:29*

Chapter 6: Judgment

God speaks concerning the judgment to come not only on Israel, but also on the Gentile nations in the writings of the prophets Jeremiah and Ezekiel, as well as in the book of Revelation.

Different world views

Today, various teachings are floating around about the End Times and the Antichrist which present a rosy future. But I believe the scriptures testify that when the Antichrist comes, the world is going to be in the midst of a catastrophe. The geography of the earth will be in shambles, the society that remains will be in chaos, and not much as we know it will be left. The majority of the Gentile nations will already have been judged severely for rejecting Jesus Christ. ITD R

Let us search the scriptures to see how I have come up with this world view or *theoryology* as I call it. *Theoryology* is comprised of Biblical facts and theory linked together.

Saved from God's Wrath

Before we continue, it's important to remember that I believe from reading God's Word that the church is saved from the coming wrath of God by the blood of Jesus Christ.

"For the *wrath of God* is revealed from heaven against all ungodliness and unrighteousness of men, who hold the truth in unrighteousness." —*Romans 1:18*

"Much more then, being now justified by his blood, *we shall be saved from wrath through him*."—*Romans 5:9*

"...even Jesus, which *delivered us from the wrath to come*."—*1 Thessalonians 1:10*

Bible Prophecy and God's Wrath

I rejoice in this deliverance but still find the question in my mind, "When does God's wrath come?" N V

Jesus, when speaking of the world wide chaos in Matthew chapter 24, stated that the generation that saw Israel reestablished would also see all scriptures fulfilled. O

"Now learn a parable of the fig tree; When his branch is yet tender, and putteth forth leaves, ye know that summer is nigh: So likewise ye, when ye shall see all these things, know that it is near, even at the doors. Verily I say unto you, *This generation shall not pass, till all these things be fulfilled*."—*Matthew 24:32–34*

Many Bible prophecies have already been fulfilled, including the birth of Christ (Isaiah 7:14) and the death of Christ as the Passover Lamb (Exodus 12:1–7 and Isaiah 53:1–12). The resurrection of Jesus is prophesied in Psalms 16:10, and Joel 2:28–32 speaks of the power of the Holy Spirit given on the day of Pentecost. All of these events were fulfilled by God's will, in the forty-second generation. The first 483 years of judgment on Israel were also fulfilled by those generations. Z J

Afterwards came the church age, the rebirth of Israel, and the retaking of Jerusalem, leaving us at the final generation, as I see it the forty-ninth generation. A few things still need to be fulfilled, including the seven years of judgment on Israel. Therefore, we can conclude that God is reestablishing Israel as a nation to deal with these seven years in the near future. L O D N

The dark side of our human nature

Both times Israel was born as a nation were preceded by acts of horror. Pharaoh, empowered by evil spirits, persecuted the Children of Israel as God prepared to bring them out of Egypt and make them a people, a great nation. Similarly, Israel's rebirth as a nation in 1948 was preceded by the holocaust visited upon the Jewish people by Hitler in World War II.

Years ago, I read the first part of Hitler's book, *Mein Kampf*. Hitler wrote that when he was in jail, angels came to him and anointed him to be ruler over all of Europe. He was a nobody at that time. Even though he ultimately failed, consider the havoc he brought to the world and to the scattered nation of Israel.

Satan and his evil forces are constantly working to destroy God's plans. Their labors are in vain for they are always thwarted in their efforts by the sovereign will of God.

For example, shortly after Jesus the Messiah was born, Satan made an attempt to kill Jesus by enticing Herod to destroy any rivals to his power, even though these supposed rivals were children. He made other attempts during the life of Christ to destroy Him, culminating with a short-lived apparent victory at His crucifixion. But the resurrection of Jesus from the dead thwarted Satan's plan to stop the redemption of man and the beginning of the church age.

Satan renewed his efforts to stop the church by his relentless persecutions of true believers beginning in Jerusalem. He then intensified his efforts by using Rome to persecute believers, and continues his diabolical work to this present day.

The point is that every time God moves, Satan counters. God is about to bring in the everlasting kingdom of Jesus Christ. In response, Satan will bring wars and destruction upon the earth.

Years ago my good friend John Broekhuizen, when comparing Herod's slaughter of the innocents to the abortion clinics of today, asked, "Who is Satan trying to kill now?" Could it be that Satan is trying to kill someone significant through the mass slaughter of infants in the abortion clinics of today?

Spiritual warfare

At the end of the Jewish captivity in Babylon, God gives us a glimpse into spiritual warfare. Cyrus, the King of Persia, allowed the Jews to go back to Judah and build their Temple as God had instructed. K

These released Jews returned to their land and began construction of the Temple. However, they were more concerned with building their own houses and establishing their own lives, so they only completed the foundation of the Temple.

About that time, the new King of Persia sent a letter that instructed the Israelites to stop building the Temple. Because of this, the people assumed it wasn't time to build the Temple. But it *was* time to build the Temple because God had already said to build it.

The people of Israel experienced consequences for not building God's house as He had told them to do. Then God raised up two anointed prophets, Zechariah and Haggai, to prophesy to the Jews.

"Then the prophets, Haggai the prophet, and Zechariah the son of Iddo, prophesied unto the Jews that were in Judah and Jerusalem in the name of the God of Israel, even unto them." *—Ezra 5:1*

Haggai prophesied concerning the physical world while Zechariah prophesied concerning spiritual warfare.

Haggai prophesied in three different months in the second year.

"Now therefore thus saith the LORD of hosts; Consider your ways. Ye have sown much, and bring in little; ye eat, but ye have not enough; ye drink, but ye are not filled with drink; ye clothe you, but there is none warm; and he that earneth wages earneth wages to put it into a bag with holes. Thus saith the LORD of hosts; Consider your ways."*—Haggai 1:5–7*

Haggai gave God's message to the Israelites. "Look, you have mildew all over your crops, your money falls out of your bags, you gather much but it disappears. Instead of building the house of God, you go to the mountains, gather wood, and build your own houses.

"You think you can do things your own way, but it's not working. I told you to build the Temple, but you have said it's not time. The Lord will restore you if you would only repent and build His house first" *(paraphrased from Haggai chapter 1).*

Finally, the people and the leaders repented and began to finish building the Temple that they had started.

Zechariah prophesied from a spiritual perspective to the same Jewish people and spoke of their complacency towards completing God's house.

"The LORD hath been sore displeased with your fathers. Therefore say thou unto them, Thus saith the LORD of hosts; Turn ye unto me, saith the LORD of hosts, and I will turn unto you, saith the LORD of hosts. Be ye not as your fathers, unto whom the former prophets have cried, saying, Thus saith the LORD of hosts; Turn ye now from your evil ways, and from your evil doings: but they did not hear, nor hearken unto me, saith the LORD."*—Zechariah 1:2-4*

In Zechariah, God also spoke of His sore displeasure at the heathen that were at ease and stated that He was returning to Jerusalem with mercies, and that His House, would be built.

"…Thus saith the LORD of hosts; I am jealous for Jerusalem and for Zion with a great jealousy. And I am *very sore displeased with the heathen* that are at ease: for I was but a little displeased, and they helped forward the affliction. Therefore thus saith the LORD; I am returned to Jerusalem with mercies: *my house shall be built* in it, saith the LORD of hosts, and a line shall be stretched forth upon Jerusalem." *—Zechariah 1:14–16*

We see the Spiritual warfare taking place around Israel in the book of Zechariah. The Lord shows Zechariah four horns. The angel tells Zechariah that the horns are the spiritual forces that have scattered Judah, Israel, and Jerusalem.

Then, Zechariah is shown four carpenters. He is told they are the spiritual forces sent to fray the horns that have destroyed Israel, Judah, and Jerusalem.

Because of similar language, I believe these are similar spirits to those of the horsemen in the seals of Revelation, who lead great, evil armies as God's judgment against Israel and against the Gentile nations—for different reasons. The judgment against Israel is to bring them to Christ. The judgment against the Gentile nations is because they rejected Christ.

To the ends of the earth

Our Lord Jesus gave instructions to His disciples which we can read in Matthew.

"… go rather to the lost sheep of the house of Israel. And as ye go, preach, saying, The kingdom of heaven is at hand. Heal the sick, cleanse the lepers, raise the dead, cast out devils:…"
—Matthew 10:6–8

"And whosoever shall not receive you, nor hear your words, when ye depart out of that house or city, *shake off the dust of your feet.*"
—Matthew 10:14

To "shake off the dust of your feet" would be a testimony against those (in this case, Israelites) who rejected the Gospel.

After His resurrection, the Lord's directive to his disciples went beyond Israel to include the Gentile nations.

"…All power is given unto me in heaven and in earth. Go ye therefore, and teach all nations, baptizing them in the name of the Father, and of the Son, and of the Holy Ghost: Teaching them to observe all things whatsoever I have commanded you…"*—Matthew 28:18–20*

These words of Christ were a testimony to the Gentile nations which would bring the nations into judgment, if they rejected the gospel.

Jesus also sent Paul to the Gentiles and told him what he was to do.

"To open their eyes, and to turn them from darkness to light, and from the power of Satan unto God, that they may receive forgiveness of sins, and inheritance among them which are sanctified by faith that is in me."*—Acts 26:18*

Paul when speaking to the Greeks at Athens, called for the Gentile nations to repent so that they could escape Judgment.

"And the times of this ignorance God winked at; but now commandeth all men every where to repent: Because he hath appointed a day, in the which he will judge the world in righteousness by that man whom he hath ordained…"*—Acts 17:30, 31*

Therefore, both Israel and the Gentile nations have been given a fair opportunity to receive Christ. This testimony will be taken into account in the day of judgment.

God's judgment on the Gentile Nations

In the past, God used the Gentile nations to judge Israel. But the Gentile nations have not experienced God's judgment and continue at ease. Jeremiah points to a future punishment of both Israel and the Gentile nations.

"Behold, the days come, saith the LORD, that I will punish all them which are circumcised *[Israel]* with the uncircumcised *[Gentiles]*." *—Jeremiah 9:25*

I see this scripture from Jeremiah being fulfilled at the time spoken of in Ezekiel chapters 38 and 39.

"And I will turn thee back, and put hooks into thy jaws, and I will bring thee forth, and all thine army, horses and horsemen, all of them clothed with all sorts of armour, even a great company with bucklers and shields, all of them handling swords."*—Ezekiel 38:4*

"And thou shalt come up against my people of Israel, as a cloud to cover the land; it shall be in the latter days, and I will bring thee against my land, that the heathen may know me, when I shall be sanctified in thee, O Gog, before their eyes."*—Ezekiel 38:16*

More evidence that connects the Gentile nations and judgment together is found in world history. When God judged Jerusalem in the twenty-eighth generation and tore it down completely, did He make all the Gentile nations drink of the cup of His fury and wrath? No. He used the Gentile nations to tear Jerusalem down! F

The next time God tore down Jerusalem in A.D. 70, did He judge all the Gentile nations with His wrath and fury? No. Again He used them to tear it down. Therefore, His fury as spoken to Jeremiah, has never been fulfilled. Yet another scripture that needs fulfillment is also found in Jeremiah. V

"Thus saith the LORD of hosts, Behold, evil shall go forth from nation to nation, and a great whirlwind shall be raised up from the coasts of the earth. And the slain of the LORD shall be at that day from one end of the earth even unto the other end of the earth: they shall not be lamented, neither gathered, nor buried; they shall be dung upon the ground." *—Jeremiah 25:32, 33*

We have had world wars, but never in connection with the judgment of Israel. But the scripture says that this will happen! As God wraps up the issue of judgment, He makes it crystal clear that no one will be spared from His cup of fury. N V

"And it shall be, if they refuse to take the cup at thine hand to drink, then shalt thou say unto them, Thus saith the LORD of hosts; Ye shall certainly drink."*—Jeremiah 25:28*

The North Country

The north country above Israel is commonly believed to be Russia, with Moscow its capital. God reveals to Ezekiel that these countries will come against Israel in the latter days and that He will be glorified because of this.

The word of the Lord came to Ezekiel.

"...set thy face against Gog, the land of Magog, the chief prince of Meshech and Tubal, and prophesy against him."*—Ezekiel 38:2*

"And thou shalt come from thy place out of the *north parts*, thou, and many people with thee, all of them riding upon horses, a great company, and a mighty army."*—Ezekiel 38:15*

This event reveals that God will deal with the Gentile nations and the last seven years of judgment on Israel at the same time. God shall bring many nations against Israel during this period of time. N

I believe that this great invading army against Israel and the conqueror of the first seal (that we will read about) are the same, and will give you my reasons for my conclusion after we identify this army.

Identify the players

Let's establish who Gog, Magog, and Tubal, mentioned in Ezekiel 38:2 are. According to the Bible, these Gentile nations are the descendants of Japheth, the son of Noah.

"The sons of Japheth; Gomer, and Magog, and Madai, and Javan, and Tubal, and Meshech, and Tiras. And the sons of Gomer; Ashkenaz, and Riphath, and Togarmah. And the sons of Javan; Elishah, and Tarshish, Kittim, and Dodanim. By these were the isles of the Gentiles divided in their lands…"—*Genesis 10:2–5*

Therefore, the nations that are against the nation of Israel are Gentile nations. Judgment now begins to fall upon the Gentile nations who come against Israel.

"And it shall come to pass at the same time when Gog shall come against the land of Israel, saith the Lord GOD, that my fury shall come up in my face. For in my jealousy and in the fire of my wrath have I spoken, Surely in that day there shall be a great shaking in the land of Israel; So that the fishes of the sea, and the fowls of the heaven, and the beasts of the field, and all creeping things that creep upon the earth, and all the men that are upon the face of the earth, shall shake at my presence, and the mountains shall be thrown down, and the steep places shall fall, and *every wall shall fall to the ground."—Ezekiel 38:18–20*

That's pretty serious isn't it? Think of all the walls in the neighborhood where you live. Think of the wall of Jerusalem where the East Gate of the Temple is located. This gate is the gate Jesus will come through when He returns, yet this too shall fall.

"Lift up your heads, O ye gates…and the King of glory shall come in."—*Psalm 24:7*

Could this be depicting Jesus standing before the collapsed East Gate ordering it to stand up again so that He could enter? That will be an exciting day to be with Jesus!

Where worlds intersect

There are two worlds, physical and spiritual. The physical world is a reflection of the events that are taking place in the spiritual world. Revelation 16:13 says that three unclean spirits like frogs come out of the mouth of the dragon, the beast, and the false prophet. It says that these spirits are devils that go forth unto the kings of the world to get them to fight in the battle of Armageddon.

Therefore, we can conclude that the spiritual action during the opening of the seals will be reflected in the natural world around us. Also, since we know that the scriptures foretell these events through prophecy, we may identify them as spiritual and not merely physical.

You'll recall my reasoning concerning spiritual warfare and its relationship to the seals; now let's look behind the first seal. What earthly events are we seeing as the first horseman goes forth with the bow in his hand?

As judgment begins

In chapter 6 of Revelation, Jesus begins to bring judgment upon Israel and the Gentile nations. Jesus the Lamb opens the first seal.

"And I saw when the Lamb opened one of the seals, and I heard, as it were the noise of thunder, one of the four beasts saying, Come and see. And I saw, and behold a white horse: and he that sat on him had a bow; and a crown was given unto him: and he went forth conquering, and to conquer."—*Revelation 6:1, 2*

Then the second seal is opened.

"And when he had opened the second seal, I heard the second beast say, Come and see. And there went out another horse that was red: and power was given to him that sat thereon to take peace from the earth, and that they should kill one another: and there was given unto him a *great sword.*"—*Revelation 6: 3, 4*

In the future, according to this second seal, the whole earth will be at war. This war is graphically depicted in the scriptures. Peace will be taken from the whole earth. Every person will be fighting. People will be killing one another worldwide.

God controls the warfare

Some people believe that the first seal is the Antichrist on a white horse with a bow in his hand. My viewpoint is that these first two horsemen are really *demonic* spirits that come out from God to do His bidding.

You may ask, "Would God allow demonic spirits to have authority?" Yes! In 1 Samuel 18:10, God allowed an evil spirit to descend upon King Saul, by which he prophesied. Also in 1 Kings chapter 22, King Ahab needed a prophet to know the future and we see that God allowed a *lying* spirit to deceive him.

God shall send a strong delusion to those who do not receive or love the truth.

"And for this cause God shall send them strong delusion, that they should believe a lie."
—*2 Thessalonians 2:11*

God does allow demonic spirits to have dominion in cases where the unrighteous have rule. God controls everything.

Remember the Bow

Remember, the first seal in Revelation chapter 6 revealed a horse. Its rider comes to *conquer with a bow in his hand.*

Let's see if this conqueror in Revelation, links with the conqueror in Ezekiel.

"And I will turn thee back, and leave but the sixth part of thee, and will cause thee to come up from the north parts, and will bring thee upon the mountains of Israel: And I will smite *thy bow out of thy left hand*, and will cause thine arrows to fall out of thy right hand."
—*Ezekiel 39:2, 3*

A person is seen carrying a bow in both Revelation 6:1, 2, and Ezekiel 39:3. Therefore, I theorize that the horseman of the first seal and the conqueror of Ezekiel chapters 38 and 39 are one and the same.

The Sword

Let's continue on to the second seal in Revelation chapter 6. God is calling for a sword against all inhabitants of the earth, provoking people to kill one another.

God calls for a sword in several verses. I believe that the sword in Revelation 6:4 and Ezekiel 38:21 are the same sword and the same event. However, if they are the same event, then we would expect to see a war on a much larger scale than merely on the mountains of Israel.

Let's see if the sword in Revelation 6:3, 4 matches with the conquering armies in Ezekiel chapter 38. As we see the conqueror coming in Ezekiel 38:21, we also see a sword accompanied by a world war.

"And I will call for a *sword* against him throughout all my mountains, saith the Lord GOD: *every man's sword* shall be against his brother."—*Ezekiel 38:21*

At this point, God has His fury in His face (Ezekiel 38:18–20). He expresses His wrath, calls for a sword, and war comes to the mountains of Israel.

The second seal judgment in Revelation states that the sword would "take peace from the earth," but in Ezekiel 38 the sword is only mentioned as taking peace from the Middle East.

Another piece to the puzzle

Let's add another piece to this puzzle and see if this war expands to a global scale. We have looked at the verses in Revelation and Ezekiel, but there is another mention of a sword in the scripture. Let's look at the series of events in Jeremiah chapter 25.

"For thus saith the LORD God of Israel unto me; Take the wine *cup of this fury* at my hand, and cause all the nations, to whom I send thee, to drink it. And they shall drink, and be moved, and be *mad, because of the sword that I will send among them.*"—*Jeremiah 25:15, 16*

Here again we find God's *fury* with the nations connected with the *sword*. Jeremiah chapter 25 identifies the nations involved in this fury and madness. The list begins with Jerusalem and escalates to encompass all the nations of the world.

"To wit, Jerusalem, and the cities of Judah, and the kings thereof, and the princes thereof, to make them a desolation, an astonishment, an hissing, and a curse; as it is this day; Pharaoh king of Egypt, and his servants, and his princes, and all his people; And all the mingled people, and all the kings of the land of Uz, and all the kings of the land of the Philistines, and Ashkelon, and Azzah, and Ekron, and the remnant of Ashdod, Edom, and Moab, and the children of Ammon, And all the kings of Tyrus, and all the kings of Zidon, and the kings of the isles which are beyond the sea, Dedan, and Tema, and Buz, and all that are in the utmost corners, And all the kings of Arabia, and all the kings of the mingled people that dwell in the desert, And all the kings of Zimri, and all the kings of Elam, and all the kings of the Medes, And all the kings of the north, far and near, one with another, and all the kingdoms of the world, which are upon the face of the earth: and the king of Sheshach shall drink after them."
—*Jeremiah 25:18–26*

With the next verse, the Lord proclaims the finality of His judgment *by this sword.*

"Therefore thou shalt say unto them, Thus saith the LORD of hosts, the God of Israel; Drink ye, and be drunken, and spue, and fall, *and rise no more*, because of the *sword* which I will send among you."—*Jeremiah 25:27*

God's Timing

God establishes the timing of this judgment.

"For, lo, I *begin* to bring evil on the city which is called by my name, and should ye be utterly unpunished? *Ye shall not be unpunished: for I will call for a sword upon all the inhabitants of the earth,* saith the LORD of hosts."—*Jeremiah 25:29*

Hundreds of years prior to Jeremiah and Ezekiel, Asaph the chief musician for King David, wrote Psalm 75. In this Psalm, he foresees the judgment of the earth.

"For in the hand of the LORD there is a cup, and the wine is red; it is full of mixture; and he poureth out of the same: but the dregs thereof, all the wicked of the earth shall wring them out, and drink them."—*Psalm 75:8*

My Scenario

With all these scriptures in mind, consider this scenario. Jesus opens the first seal and the invading armies mentioned in Ezekiel chapter 38 come against Israel. He then opens the second seal and releases a sword that expands this war from Israel to the whole world. It starts locally and escalates globally. I believe this global expansion of the conflict is evidenced by Ezekiel.

"And I will send a fire on Magog, and among them that dwell carelessly in the isles: and they shall know that I am the LORD. So will I make my holy name known in the midst of my people Israel; and I will not let them pollute my holy name any more: and the heathen shall know that I am the LORD, the Holy One in Israel." —*Ezekiel 39:6, 7*

Again the question: Why?

As you can see, the whole world will come under this judgment. Why? The answer is obvious, for I don't think the Gentile nations can continue to defy the witness of the Holy Spirit and not be held accountable. V

For example, abortions are uncontrolled, crime is everywhere, and immorality is commonplace. Sin has been declared a civil right. Just consider the heinous sin of homosexuality. Do you think that the Gentile nations can continue to say that homosexuality is right and the Bible is wrong and not be judged by their words? This immoral act is as sinful today as it was in the time of Sodom and Gomorrah.

Consider homosexuality for a moment. Proponents are trying to convince us that homosexuality is a mental or genetic disorder. Secular studies claim that there is something different about the homosexual brain. I'm sure they are right for God said there would be something different about them, but it is not a birth defect, it is a moral decision.

"And even as they did not like to retain God in their knowledge, God gave them over to a reprobate mind, to do those things which are not convenient."—*Romans 1:28*

God turns people who practice this sin over to reprobate minds, minds without judgment; corrupt, and immoral. In fact, this sin is the last straw.

To illuminate one such occasion, look at Joshua as he led the Children of Israel into the promised land. He was directed by God to drive the inhabitants off the land for their sins had come to fullness (Genesis 15:13–16). Their long history of unrepentant sin had progressed to the accepting of homosexuality as a way of life, which in turn led to the despicable sin of bestiality. These sins were about to cause the land to *vomit off* its inhabitants. Joshua and his army was the instrument that God was about to use to fulfill His judgment.

"Thou shalt not lie with mankind, as with womankind: it is abomination. Neither shalt thou lie with any beast to defile thyself therewith: neither shall any woman stand before a beast to lie down thereto: it is confusion. Defile not ye yourselves in any of these things: for in all these the nations are defiled which I cast out before you: And the land is defiled: therefore I do visit the iniquity thereof upon it, and the land itself vomiteth out her inhabitants. Ye shall therefore keep my statutes and my judgments, and shall not commit any of these abominations; neither any of your own nation, nor any stranger that sojourneth among you: (For all these abominations have the men of the land done, which were before you, and the land is defiled;) That the land spue not you out also, when ye defile it, as it spued out the nations that were before you. For whosoever shall commit any of these abominations, even the souls that commit them shall be cut off from among their people."—*Leviticus 18:22–29*

If homosexuality was genetic, then God would be unjust in judging these as well as the people of Sodom and Gomorrah. It's not a genetic disease. It is a sinful choice, made by a sinful nature. The sin of homosexuality needs to be repented of just like any other sin, whether it be stealing, lying, adultery, or fornication. However, the Bible makes a distinction with the sin of homosexuality, in that it has national consequences.

The Apostle Peter, and Jude (the half-brother of Jesus), proclaimed judgment on nations that are given over to this sin in their epistles.

"And turning the cities of Sodom and Gomorrha into ashes condemned them with an overthrow, making them an ensample unto those that after should live ungodly."—*2 Peter 2:6*

"Even as Sodom and Gomorrha, and the cities about them in like manner, giving themselves over to fornication, and going after strange flesh, are set forth for an example, suffering the vengeance of eternal fire."—*Jude 1:7*

The sin of homosexuality even produces judgment in a transgressor's body.

"Wherefore God also gave them up to uncleanness through the lusts of their own hearts, to dishonour their own bodies between themselves: Who changed the truth of God into a lie, and worshipped and served the creature more than the Creator, who is blessed for ever. Amen. For this cause God gave them up unto vile affections: for even their women did change the natural use into that which is against nature: And likewise also the men, leaving the natural use of the woman, burned in their lust one toward another; men with men working that which is unseemly, and *receiving in themselves that recompence of their error which was meet."—Romans 1:24–27*

Judgment for rejecting the Gospel

Immorality is sufficient reason for God's judgment to fall on the Gentile nations. But the rejection of the Gospel is the underlying cause for God's judgment.

"And ye shall be brought before governors and kings for my sake, *for a testimony against them and the Gentiles."—Matthew 10:18*

"He that believeth on him is not condemned: but he that believeth not is condemned already, because he hath not believed in the name of the only begotten Son of God."—*John 3:18*

Today, the Gentile nations and the western world appear to be in political, economic, and military control. Wall Street appears successful, and Madison Avenue has tricked us into believing that happiness is just around the corner and within our reach. In contemporary Christianity, the future is commonly depicted as a time of peace and prosperity.

However, I don't believe the End Times will be this way. My theoryology is that the Gentile nations will be devastated through war. Then the Antichrist will rule Israel and what's left of the Gentile nations for seven years. The Temple will be rebuilt, and the Antichrist will put his idol in it, proclaiming himself to be God. ITD

As we have seen in *Chapter 5: Cause of Remaining Judgment*, the Gentiles have nothing to do with the *sins of Manasseh*, therefore, they don't come under that judgment. However, they will be judged for their rejection of the *Light* (Jesus Christ).

The walk of the believer

The believer's sins have already been judged at the cross of Calvary. When we participate in communion, we remember that the penalty for sins, which is death, was paid by Jesus' death on the cross. We have been justified (acquitted) by the resurrection of Jesus and celebrate our freedom from the coming judgment and wrath of God because of the shed blood of Jesus on that same cross.

"For as often as ye eat this bread, and drink this cup, ye do shew the Lord's death till he come."—*1 Corinthians 11:26*

Therefore, each time we take communion, we as believers examine ourselves concerning the blood of Jesus Christ. We take communion worthily (honestly and with an open heart towards God) to avoid being *guilty of the body and blood of Jesus Christ.* Q

"Wherefore whosoever shall eat this bread, and drink this cup of the Lord, unworthily, shall be *guilty of the body and blood of the Lord.* But let a man examine himself, and so let him eat of that bread, and drink of that cup."
—*1 Corinthians 11:27, 28*

If we as believers do not examine ourselves, and continue to live in sin, we subject ourselves to God's chastisement.

"For he that eateth and drinketh unworthily, eateth and drinketh damnation to himself, not discerning the Lord's body. For this cause many are weak and sickly among you, and many sleep."—*1 Corinthians 11:29-30*

"For the time is come that judgment must begin at the house of God: and if it first begin at us, what shall the end be of them that obey not the gospel of God? And if the righteous scarcely be saved, where shall the ungodly and the sinner appear?"—*1 Peter 4:17, 18*

"Examine yourselves, whether ye be in the faith…"—*2 Corinthians 13:5*

Part of this self-examination before God is to walk in the light (1 John 1:7). If we find ourselves in sin, God has the solution.

"If we confess our sins, he is faithful and just to forgive us our sins, and to cleanse us from all unrighteousness."—*I John 1:9*

If you fail to do these simple things, God will help you through His correction, *but He always keeps you under the blood of Jesus.* If you stray away, He'll find you and bring you back to save you from the wrath that is to come on the earth. Q S

"But when we are judged, we are chastened of the Lord, that we should not be condemned with the world."—*1 Corinthians 11:32*

This is all accomplished because of His unmerited love for us (grace), not because of our works.

We are at the end of the Gentile era

As we end this chapter, I want to leave you with a closing thought. In our day and age, a world war over the Middle East is not only likely, it is imminent. I am sure that this judgment on the nation of Israel and the Gentile nations will be preceded by the deliverance of the believers from God's wrath.

Now that Jerusalem is part of Israel, we know that the end of the Gentile era has begun. O

"And they shall fall by the edge of the sword, and shall be led away captive into all nations: and Jerusalem shall be trodden down of the Gentiles, until the times of the Gentiles be fulfilled."—Luke 21:24

We are now waiting for the fullness of the Gentiles to come in.

"For I would not, brethren, that ye should be ignorant of this mystery, lest ye should be wise in your own conceits; that blindness in part is happened to Israel, *until the fulness of the Gentiles be come in."—Romans 11:25*

We know for sure it's time to look up—for our Redeemer is coming! D W

"And when these things begin to come to pass, then *look up*, and lift up your heads; for your redemption draweth nigh."—*Luke 21:28*

"Be not afraid of sudden fear, neither of the desolation of the wicked, when it cometh. For the LORD shall be thy confidence, and shall keep thy foot from being taken."
—*Proverbs 3:25, 26*

"With my soul have I desired thee in the night; yea, with my spirit within me will I seek thee early: for when thy judgments are in the earth, the inhabitants of the world will learn righteousness."
—Isaiah 26:9

Chapter 7: The Church Age

The Gentile nations did not know the way to God until Paul the apostle began preaching about Jesus Christ to the people of Asia Minor and Europe.

A time will come again when the Gentile nations will have no knowledge of Jesus Christ. When the church is removed there will be no more evidence of the love of Christ. At that time, God will focus his attention on the nation of Israel, who turned their backs on Him. W S

Recently, there has been a stirring spiritually in Israel, and Jewish people are receiving Jesus as their Messiah more than ever before. There are hundreds of Messianic fellowships springing up across the land of Israel, and revival seems to be taking place among the underdeveloped nations worldwide as well.

At the same time, there is a falling away from God's Word in the churches of the European Union (EU), and in the United States. Many denominations are rapidly moving away from the teaching of His Word, even ordaining and marrying homosexuals.

The larger non-denominational churches are using methods taken from corporate America to bring people to their congregations. These corporate centers are replacing good Bible translations with unscriptural, paraphrased Bibles. One of these paraphrased books replaces the words "Lord Jesus" with the phrase "master Jesus," a new-age term.

The author of one paraphrase revealed his contempt for the Word of God by stating on record that Bible study and the study of prophecy is unnecessary and counter-productive in a believer's life, even though the Bible clearly states that study is necessary.

"Study to shew thyself approved unto God, a workman that needeth not to be ashamed, rightly dividing the word of truth."
—2 Timothy 2:15

These same churches forbid the study of prophecy. Many conform to *replacement theology* that states that the church has replaced Israel, and that Israel is the problem in the world today. It's not hard to see that the church's influence is declining in America; just consider its departure from steadfastness in God's Word. Furthermore, the church is supposed to be the pillar and ground of truth in society.

For example, recently it was made public that a well-known pastor who led millions of evangelicals in a semi-political movement and took strong stands against sodomite (homosexual) marriages was outed by his sodomite partner. A short time later, another pastor of another large church in the same town resigned for the same reason. As the church goes, so goes society.

"But if I tarry long, that thou mayest know how thou oughtest to behave thyself in the house of God, which is the church of the living God, the pillar and ground of the truth."—*1 Timothy 3:15*

So we see the church replacing and rejecting the sure foundation of God's Word with paraphrased editions that lean toward Eastern Mysticism. And as the church substitutes secular wisdom for evangelism, society rejects God's absolute truth. As a result, believers shouldn't be surprised when talk show hostesses bring their lesbian partners on the air with them. As the church goes, so goes society, and so goes the nation. This condition can be summed up with two verses from Malachi.

"Ye have said, It is vain to serve God: and what profit is it that we have kept his ordinance, and that we have walked mournfully before the LORD of hosts? And now we call the proud happy; yea, they that work wickedness are set up; yea, they that tempt God are even delivered."—*Malachi 3:14–15*

The Sceptre

While visiting Israel in March of 1995, I stood upon the top of Masada, a plateau which overlooks the Dead Sea, and listened to our tour guide relate the story of the nation of Israel's terrible ending in A.D. 70. The Temple had been destroyed by the Roman General, Titus. The remaining Jews had fled to this mountain top in order to try to survive as a nation. M

This wretched remnant of the once great Judah was now surrounded by Roman forces. Perhaps you've read one of the books written about Masada. If you have, you know the story. Instead of accepting surrender and slavery, these Jews chose mass suicide to thwart the intentions of the cruel Romans.

After listening to this account given by our guide, the Lord brought a scripture to my mind. At that instant I realized why this insignificant mountain, with its few insignificant refugees, meant so much to the Jewish nation and to their knowledge of their Messiah. I then understood why Israel publicized the history of Masada so much.

If Masada hadn't taken place, the Jews would have made peace with the Romans and lived under their authority. If the Jews had ruled their own nation as a puppet state of Rome, the scripture given in Genesis chapter 49 could not have been fulfilled.

"The sceptre shall not depart from Judah, nor a lawgiver from between his feet, until Shiloh come; and unto him shall the gathering of the people be."—*Genesis 49:10*

I have come to believe that this event at Masada was actually the sceptre departing from Judah. The lawgiver in this scripture was the Temple and its priesthood. When the Babylonian Captivity took place and the Temple was destroyed the first time, the sceptre (the authority to rule) did not depart from Judah. Judah did not lose the "lawgiver from between his feet" during the first captivity, because the priesthood continued. In fact, upon Judah's return from the Babylonian captivity, Joshua the son of Jozadak was the High Priest (lawgiver) that returned with the governor, Zerubbabel, the son of Shealtiel. I

When the Romans destroyed the Temple in A.D. 70, they also destroyed the priesthood. Therefore, the lawgiver departed from Judah. Genesis 49:10 says that these two events would not happen *until Shiloh came*. Any Jewish scholar will tell you that *Shiloh* is the first name for the Messiah that was first promised to Adam and Eve in the Old Testament in Genesis 3:15. M

If at Masada the lawgiver was taken and the sceptre departed from Judah, then the nation of Israel has to accept that the Messiah came to Israel before A.D. 70 because Masada says to all Israel and to all the world that Judah had lost its sceptre!

The New Covenant begins

Before the fulfilling of this scripture from Genesis, God launched the early church by the outpouring of the Holy Spirit and the anointed teaching of His apostles in Jerusalem.

On the road to Damascus, Jesus gave Paul God's plan for reaching the Gentile world with His Word.

"...open their eyes, and to turn them from darkness to light, and from the power of Satan unto God, that they may receive forgiveness of sins, and inheritance among them which are sanctified by faith that is in me."—*Acts 26:18*

Later, the directive was clarified by James, the half brother of Jesus and the first Bishop of the church in the book of Acts.

"...Men and brethren, hearken unto me: Simeon hath declared how God at the first did visit the Gentiles, to take out of them a people for his name."—*Acts 15:13, 14*

The Gentile church was instituted not as a replacement for Israel, but as an effort by God to save all of the descendants of Adam and Eve through Noah and all of his sons. This included the descendants of Japheth and Ham, along with the children of Shem. Paul, the apostle to the Gentiles, tells why blindness happened to the Jews in the book of Romans.

"...blindness in part is happened to Israel, until the fulness of the Gentiles be come in. And so all Israel shall be saved..."—*Romans 11:25, 26*

Commonwealth—two become one

Paul gives us more insight into God's plan for redeeming the race of Adam and Eve in Ephesians chapter 2, by telling us that the Jews and the Gentiles are one in Christ. When God is finished taking "a people for his namesake" (Acts 15:14) from the Gentile nations, and making them partakers of the promise to Abraham, he will turn His attention back to Israel. Sight will return to Israel and they will recognize their Messiah. That day on Masada was a great day in my life, for I understood why so many people visit there and the Jews are so captivated with this place.

Prophetic letters to the Church

Now let's turn our attention to the church age. The apostle John wrote the book of Revelation in A.D. 90. The first three chapters contain seven letters to seven churches in Asia that Jesus instructed John to write. L

These seven letters are viewed by many believers and Bible teachers as prophetic statements about church history, the time of the Gentiles, or the church age. There are very clear parallels between the history of Christianity, past, present, and future, and what was written in the seven letters to the seven churches. L

The letters begin with the church of *Ephesus*, stating that the initial church age had lost its first love. As time passed, the persecution of the church came upon the age of *Smyrna*. Around the year A.D. 300, the age of *Pergamos*, Satan brought his seat of authority into the church. This situation has continued even until today. L

Then the dark age of *Thyatira* raised its ugly head and brought full-blown idolatry into Christianity. This idolatrous church remains visible today. The Renaissance ushered in *Sardis*, the *dead* church, which claimed new light, but was in darkness. The next age, *Philadelphia,* was the *alive* church.

Laodicea, the last age, is the lukewarm church. The transition to this lukewarm church is characterized by preaching which mixes a worldly and material gospel with the traditions from the idolatrous age, Thyatira (Revelation, chapters 2–3).

False Enlightenment

Sardis, I believe, was the *Renaissance* Church which embraced *false enlightenment*, and had a reputation for being alive. As the Dark Ages faded, this idolatrous church boasted of new enlightenment. But it wasn't enlightenment about God and about Jesus Christ. Instead it was *secular humanism* that came into the church mainly through the writings of Thomas Aquinas. L

If you study the writings of Aquinas, you will see that he took the writings of Aristotle and other Greek scholars and mixed them with the teachings of Christ. This was the beginning of Secular Humanism that eventually worked its way into Christianity.

Aquinas' writings are beautiful and flowery. They appear to be inspired by God, but in reality are rooted in satanism. Basically, Aquinas believed that when Adam and Eve fell, they only fell spiritually, keeping their intellect intact. This opened the door for the mixing of the writings of ancient, pagan scholars, and the Word of God. Comparing these writings to the doctrines of Jesus Christ (Revelation 3:1–6) reveals how truly blasphemous they really are.

The True Light

The church of Philadelphia was and is the excited church. It is a church that doesn't deny the name of Jesus nor deny His Word. This church is going to be *kept* from the Great Tribulation that is going to come upon all the earth. I believe that the time of the alive church of Philadelphia started with the Reformation, but today all that's left is a remnant.

The Reformation started when men and women began to think freely again, and came back to the simplicity of God's Word and faith in Jesus Christ alone. L

"…The just shall live by faith."—*Habakkuk 2:4, Romans 1:17, Galations 3:11, Hebrews 10:38*

I believe that the great nation of the United States was formed by *Reformists* as they fled from the persecution of the Renaissance Church of southern Europe. Today, the Philadelphia or Reformists' church still clings to life and will be kept from the hour of Tribulation coming on all the world.

"And to the angel of the church in Philadelphia write; These things saith he that is holy, he that is true, he that hath the key of David, he that openeth, and no man shutteth; and shutteth, and no man openeth; I know thy works: behold, I have set before thee an open door, and no man can shut it: for thou hast a little strength, and *hast kept my word*, and *hast not denied my name*. Behold, I will make them of the

synagogue of Satan, which say they are Jews, and are not, but do lie; behold, I will make them to come and worship before thy feet, and to know that I have loved thee. *Because thou hast kept the word of my patience, I also will keep thee from the hour of temptation, which shall come upon all the world, to try them that dwell upon the earth.* Behold, I come quickly: hold that fast which thou hast, that no man take thy crown. Him that overcometh will I make a pillar in the temple of my God, and he shall go no more out: and I will write upon him the name of my God, and the name of the city of my God, which is new Jerusalem, which cometh down out of heaven from my God: and I will write upon him my new name. He that hath an ear, let him hear what the Spirit saith unto the churches."
—*Revelation 3:7-13* L

Tepid Christianity

Laodicea, the *lukewarm* church will seek to combine the lusts of the world with Christianity. They will be wealthy and in need of nothing, except something to cover their shame. L

"…thou sayest, I am rich, and increased with goods, and have need of nothing; and knowest not that thou art wretched, and miserable, and poor, and blind, and naked."—*Revelation 3:17*

The only way you can be *spiritually blind* in the New Testament is if Satan blinds you.

"In whom the *god of this world hath blinded the minds of them which believe not*, lest the light of the glorious gospel of Christ, who is the image of God, should shine unto them."
—*2 Corinthians 4:4*

Lies, lies, lies

Satan is the father of liars and his lies cause spiritual blindness. As men continue in darkness God will allow the lie to take hold. In fact, He will send it to those who have rejected His son.

"And for this cause God shall send them strong delusion, that they should believe a lie."
—*2 Thessalonians 2:11*

I believe that the Laodicean church is here now. We can recognize this lukewarm church by the worldly doctrines that have infiltrated modern day Christianity, diluting Biblical truths, and blinding the eyes of people. These teachings are contrary to Jesus Christ and what He said in God's Word.

Doctrines that say Jesus was an angel or the brother of Satan, that riches won't corrupt you, and that you should seek wealth as a confirmation of God's blessing, are corrupt and not from the Holy Spirit.

The Emergent Church we see today is characterized by a return to icons, candles, idol worship, and contemporary marketing techniques, rather than being led by the Spirit of God. We also see tolerance and political correctness in the church today, along with the watering down of God's Word. These are clear indicators that the church is on a very slippery slope to reprobation. These doctrines from Satan are intended to dilute the truth and blind the eyes of people.

Our real teacher

The erroneous teachings that are rampant today testify that Satan is working hard trying to destroy Christianity. That is why you should not rely upon the teachings of any man or woman, including myself.

"But the anointing which ye have received of him abideth in you, and *ye need not that any man teach you:* but as the same anointing teacheth you of all things, and is truth, and is no lie, and even as it hath taught you, ye shall abide in him."—*1 John 2:27*

The only thing you really need to grow in Christ is a personal knowledge of the Word of God. Study the Bible from cover to cover and rely on the Holy Spirit to lead and teach you.

The two-fold sign of the end of the age

We see in Luke chapter 21 that the sign for the end of the Gentile Church Age is two-fold. O

"... and shall be led away captive into all nations: and Jerusalem shall be trodden down of the Gentiles, until the times of the Gentiles be fulfilled."—*Luke 21:24*

This verse says that Israel would be scattered and that Jerusalem would be under Gentile control *until* the church age was fulfilled or nearing its end. Therefore, Israel would be made a nation and Jerusalem would come under Jewish control. L

Israel became a nation in 1948, and Jerusalem was made part of Israel on June 8, 1967, fulfilling the very words of Christ. The blindness of Israel is coming to an end as the fullness of the Gentiles nears completion. O

"For I would not, brethren, that ye should be ignorant of this mystery, lest ye should be wise in your own conceits; that blindness in part is happened to Israel, *until the fulness of the Gentiles be come in*."—*Romans 11:25*

Again, as we see the current revival going on in Israel, we also see the diminishing of true Christianity among most of the Gentile nations which Paul writes about in 2 Thessalonians.

"Now we beseech you, brethren, by the coming of our Lord Jesus Christ, and by our gathering together unto him, That ye be not soon shaken in mind, or be troubled, neither by spirit, nor by word, nor by letter as from us, as that the day of Christ is at hand. Let no man deceive you by any means: for that day shall not come, except there come a falling away first, and that man of sin be revealed, the son of perdition." —*2 Thessalonians 2:1–3*

The falling away was written concerning the Gentile church. Israel had already fallen away when this was written.

The roles reverse

When Israel fell away, the Gentile church was grafted in like a wild olive branch. My belief is that everything will now reverse. The Gentile Church will diminish as Israel grows and strengthens spiritually.

In the End Times, as the Gentile Church loses its sight, Israel will regain its sight (Romans 11:25). ITD

These events are happening today, thereby leading me to the conclusion that the end of the Gentile era is upon us. Soon there will be a *fullness* of the Gentile Church and the church age will be over.

Time to consider

Maybe you are reading this and don't know Jesus Christ as your personal Saviour. Right now, at this moment, you have an opportunity to accept Jesus Christ as your personal Saviour.

Stop reading and take some time and pray. If you are unsure of your salvation (your position with God) all you need to do is speak to God the Father and admit you are lost, a sinner, and need to be forgiven for your deeds. Ask Him to cleanse you and bring you to the saving knowledge of Jesus and His sacrifice for your sins. Tell Him you want to start fresh as a new person. Tell Him you want to be born again. Suppose that you are the last Gentile to complete His plan. If that is true, if you are the last Gentile, expect the Lord to come for His Church as soon as you accept the Lord!

If you are saved and realize the urgency of the times, then it's time to put this book down for a while and set your face toward the Lord for direction in your life.

"But the day of the Lord will come as a thief in the night; in the which the heavens shall pass away with a great noise, and the elements shall melt with fervent heat, the earth also and the works that are therein shall be burned up. *Seeing then that all these things shall be dissolved, what manner of persons ought ye to be in all holy conversation and godliness,* Looking for and hasting unto the coming of the day of God, wherein the heavens being on fire shall be dissolved, and the elements shall melt with fervent heat?"—*2 Peter 3:10–12*

"But thou, O man of God, flee these things; and *follow after righteousness, godliness, faith, love, patience, meekness."—1 Timothy 6:11*

"And when these things begin to come to pass, *then look up*, and lift up your heads; for your redemption draweth nigh."—*Luke 21:28*

Chapter 8: The Last Generation

The last generation began when Israel became a nation in 1948, and it will end at the Second Coming of Jesus Christ. It still remains for Israel to build a Temple so the Antichrist can have a place to put the Abomination of Desolation. D H T

The first abomination, placed in the Temple by Manasseh, son of King Hezekiah (see *Chapter 5: Cause of Remaining Judgment*), brought about God's judgment of desolation and destruction on Jerusalem. G

The abomination that causes desolation before Jesus' Second Coming, is the placing of the Antichrist's idol in the Temple. This will bring God's wrath and destruction on the Antichrist and his army. H

Moving towards the building of the Temple

Revelation was written by the apostle John in A.D. 90, twenty years *after* the Temple was destroyed in A.D. 70. This means that there remains another future Temple that will be built to fulfill the scripture in the book of Revelation. M

"And there was given me a reed like unto a rod: and the angel stood, saying, Rise, and measure the temple of God, and the altar, and them that worship therein. But the court which is without the temple leave out, and measure it not; for it is given unto the Gentiles: and the holy city shall they tread under foot forty and two months."
—*Revelation 11:1, 2*

Currently, there are several Jewish organizations in Israel preparing for the rebuilding of the Temple. The *Temple Institute* is busy preparing all the garments, instruments, and tools that are necessary in the daily administration of the priest. Another group, *The Temple Mount Faithful*, have already cut the cornerstone for the Temple and have placed it in a vacant field, waiting for the day when the building begins and the cornerstone will be placed on Mount Moriah.

Time of destruction—Time of the announcement

Daniel prophesied that the Antichrist will place his image in the Holy of Holies and declare himself to be God. Therefore, there is a future temple that remains to be built. H

"...and they shall pollute the sanctuary of strength, and shall take away the daily sacrifice, and they shall place the abomination that maketh desolate."—*Daniel 11:31*

"Who opposeth and exalteth himself above all that is called God, or that is worshipped; so that he as God sitteth in the temple of God, shewing himself that he is God."—*2 Thessalonians 2:4*

"But *when ye shall see the abomination of desolation*, spoken of by Daniel the prophet, standing where it ought not, (*let him that readeth understand,*) then let them that be in Judaea flee to the mountains."—*Mark 13:14* H

"That seeing they may see, and not perceive; and hearing they may hear, and not understand; lest at any time they should be converted, and their sins should be forgiven them."—*Mark 4:12*

Jesus explains here that the only way someone can understand the Word of God is if they are spiritually converted and their sins are forgiven. Paul also talks about the natural man who can not understand spiritual things.

"But the natural man receiveth not the things of the Spirit of God: for they are foolishness unto him: neither can he know them, because they are spiritually discerned."—*1 Corinthians 2:14*

You must be Born Again

If you are not *born again,* that is, *spiritually converted and your sins forgiven*, you are a natural man or woman and the Word of God will not make sense to you. It will merely be just another book filled with so many words.

When Jesus says, "Let him that readeth understand," He is speaking about people that know the Lord. All scripture will become clear to believers that apply their hearts to seek the Lord in His Word.

To illustrate this, recently I watched a television program aired by a station owned and operated by a university that used a secular and humanistic educational format. An instructor was lecturing on how to discover your inner being. His lecture was based on, "He that loses his life shall find it," an incomplete scripture quotation. Both the instructor and the audience found this scripture to be humorous. The instructor used a fictional story to illustrate his interpretation of the partial quotation.

There was a child who wanted to be a violinist. However, his counselors and parents talked him into being a lawyer instead. This child grew up and worked as a lawyer all his life. Suddenly and tragically, he developed cancer and only had one more year to live. He then became a violinist and suddenly his cancer went away. The instructor concluded, "This is how to lose your life to find it."

This example illustrates how the natural man cannot understand the things of God. The instructor's interpretation of the Word of God was incorrect. His analogy had nothing to do with the shortened scripture he used.

"He that findeth his life shall lose it: and he that loseth his life *for my sake* shall find it."
—*Matthew 10:39*

If you read the complete verse, you will understand that Jesus was actually describing how to follow Him and be his disciple.

"…If any man will come after me, let him deny himself, and take up his cross, and follow me."—*Matthew 16:24*

The spiritual man would understand this to mean we need to make Jesus and His ambitions and goals first in our lives. When we make Him the Lord of our lives, we really find the life that He has designed for us.

Those who flee

Now that we have established who can read and understand, it is important to identify who it is that is to flee to the mountains when they see the abomination of desolation. In Mark 13:14, Jesus is specifically speaking to the people of Judea that understand—*Messianic Jews.* H

These Jews, through the testimony of the two witnesses (see *Chapter 10: The Order of Things*), come to believe that Jesus is the Messiah after the deliverance of believers from judgment through the redemption of the Church. These must be the ones who will read and understand the scriptural admonition during the tribulation period, and will "flee to the mountains." N W

The Elect

In Matthew, Jesus comments on the shortening of days for the elect's sake.

"And except those days should be shortened, there should no flesh be saved: but for the elect's sake those days shall be shortened." —*Matthew 24:22*

Again, I believe the elect in this instance are the Messianic Jews. These are the ones who can read and understand, and are living in Judea. This scripture is not referring to anyone in the United States, Europe, or any place other than Judea. These are the elect at that particular time. They didn't deserve it, but they are the elect by His grace—believers chosen and called by God. Salvation is not something anyone earns or merits. N

Road signs

Along with the sign of the building of the Temple, Jesus said other signs would appear that would alert the believer that His coming was near. We are alerted to two of these signs as we observe the societies of earth take on the attributes of the days of Noah and Lot.

"And as it was in the *days of Noe*, so shall it be also in the days of the Son of man.—*Luke 17:26*

"And GOD saw that the wickedness of man was great in the earth, and that every imagination of the thoughts of his heart was only evil continually."—*Genesis 6:5*

"The earth also was corrupt before God, and the earth was filled with violence...for all flesh had corrupted his way upon the earth." —*Genesis 6:11, 12*

"Likewise also as it was in *the days of Lot*..." —*Luke 17:28*

"...the men of Sodom were wicked and sinners before the LORD exceedingly."—*Genesis 13:13*

"And the LORD said, Because the cry of Sodom and Gomorrah is great, and because their sin is very grievous; I will go down now, and see whether they have done altogether according to the cry of it, which is come unto me; and if not, I will know."—*Genesis 18:20, 21*

There weren't even ten righteous people in the city of Sodom.

"Peradventure ten shall be found there. And he said, I will not destroy it for ten's sake." —*Genesis 18:32*

The people of the days of Noah and the days of Lot continued on in their daily lives and immoral lifestyle disregarding God's ways, oblivious to His warnings of judgment to come.

"And as it was in the days of Noe, so shall it be also in the days of the Son of man. They did eat, they drank, they married wives, they were given in marriage, until the day that Noe entered into the ark, and the flood came, and destroyed them all. Likewise also as it was in the days of Lot; they did eat, they drank, they bought, they sold, they planted, they builded."
—Luke 17:26–28

World government and the loss of country sovereignty

In our world today there are individuals and organizations emerging that promote a new world order where all nations will join together under the banner of tolerance and world peace. This world government would include free trade, and acceptance of all people and all religions as the same and equal. Included in this group are those that are considered to be Christian leaders, part of the deception of this age that Jesus warned repeatedly about.

Tolerance and world peace sound good, but beneath the surface, the believer sees the rise of the fourth kingdom mentioned in Daniel chapter 7. H

The tragic events of September 11, 2001, when the World Trade Towers and Pentagon were attacked, have helped to soften the resistance to the idea of a New World Order. The 911 attacks also engaged us in a struggle between two great world views—that of the Middle East and that of the West. The differences between the two world views is greater than can be solved by merely adopting religious tolerance, however.

Our hard-won freedom that we enjoy in the United States and the freedom we are supposedly fighting for in the world is being attacked from countries driven by religious fanaticism. Our freedom is also being undermined from within our own nation. How can a new order arise out of a world that is so torn by hatred and opposing ideologies?

We speak of the attack as the beginning of a long war on terrorism. Perhaps it is, and rightfully so. However, in the name of national security, the western governments have enacted extreme procedures that compromise freedom. This includes things like national ID cards, increased surveillance, and programs that compromise personal privacy. A false sense of security could also be promoted by a national health plan, where the government promises to care for its citizens from the cradle to the grave. But this increased protection comes at a high price. Because of higher taxes, we end up with less disposable income, and less personal freedom.

Government controls are replacing freedom, and the transition towards world government becomes easier, all in the name of peace and safety. Those who exchange freedom for security end up with neither.

Peace and safety

Paul talks about the signs of the last generation, destruction, and the Lord's coming. D

"But of the times and the seasons, brethren, ye have no need that I write unto you. For yourselves know perfectly that the day of the Lord so cometh as a thief in the night. For when they shall say, *Peace and safety*; then sudden destruction cometh upon them, as travail upon a woman with child; and they shall not escape."*—1 Thessalonians 5:1–3*

In the name of peace and safety, we are also witnessing the movement towards regionalism and away from nationalism. For example, it is evident that the United States,

Canada, and Mexico are in the process of being combined into one region. This is a step towards the One World Government prophesied in the Bible so long ago. N

Bible believers who love the truth will not be deceived, but if the true church speaks out against sin and false peace in this new world, it will be accused of hate speech, hate crimes, or being unpatriotic. The truth will be treated as intolerance, or a lie, and the lie of world peace could be treated as the truth in this upside-down new world order.

The word you hear in every political campaign is *safety* which is interpreted by the voters as *prosperity*. Promises of removing barriers to world trade promote the idea that all can be rich. The National ID cards increase the sense of personal safety along with many other promises. All of these ideas promoting the world's idea of peace and safety are part of the strong delusion.

The whole world hopes for peace and safety, but rejects the true peace that only comes from Jesus.

Don't yield to this sign

Around the time of the first publication of this book in the early '90s, I read an article concerning how some of our tax money was used in America. The National Endowment for the Arts announced that it would fund three homosexual film festivals in Los Angeles, New York, and Pittsburgh. The content matter of the featured films is too grotesque to describe. With no regard to decency, these festivals violated our traditional and moral standards.

Our government uses our tax money to fund the National Endowment of the Arts. That means *We The People* are supporting sodomy.

Now, more than ten years after this book was first written, the same immoral film festivals would not even make the news. Our society has become far more tolerant and more insensitive to sin. Currently the United States issues marriage licenses to homosexual couples in a growing number of states. What's next? To see the progression of sin, read Leviticus 18:1–25. Are we inching towards legalized bestiality? Is that the ultimate objective of the sodomites?

Jesus said sodomy would prevail in the End Times, just as it did in the last days of Lot in the cities of Sodom and Gomorrah. Keep looking up. Jesus is not far away from judging this degradation. He said this would precede His Second Coming. ITD

"But the same day that Lot went out of Sodom it rained fire and brimstone from heaven, and destroyed them all. Even *thus shall it be in the day when the Son of man is revealed.*"
—Luke 17:29, 30

Would you have thought you'd ever see a generation change so much? History books will tell you of periods of time that sin abounded in society. But you do not read about this abounding sin happening in conjunction with Israel becoming a nation. *You do now!* O

Everything will be all right—Just hug a tree

Some environmental organizations say that Bible-believing Christians are responsible for the anti-environment movement in the world. They think Christians are more interested in saving souls than they are trees, water, and air. They are really looking for a scapegoat to pin the blame on.

The fact of the matter is that Bible-believing Christians are pro-environment in the sense that they respect the earth as God's creation. Our earth is actually being destroyed by greed and the lust for power, not soul winning. Revelation does say that there will be judgment on those that destroy the earth.

"And the nations were angry, and thy wrath is come, and the time of the dead, that they should be judged, ... *and that thou shouldest destroy them which destroy the earth.*"
—Revelation 11:18

A safe, nuclear-free world?

We have seen the collapse of the Soviet Union and have been reassured that their nuclear warheads are now in safe hands. Our leaders want us to believe that the world is a safer place now that the cold war is over.

However, since the collapse of the Soviet Union, many more countries have come into the nuclear club. At the time of this writing, Iran, North Korea, and Al Qaeda now have nuclear weapons. See *Appendix B—Nuclear Proliferation Chart* for a shocking look at the proliferation of the world's nuclear arsenal.

The Scriptures and the atom

When I was in the military back in the fifties, I was trained in bomb disposal in Explosive Ordinance Disposal School. As a technician, I was trained to defuse bombs that didn't go off. I was also trained in demolition at the same school. Part of the nuclear training also included an intense course in Nuclear Physics that was put together for the military by MIT.

The way a nuclear weapon works is not classified information anymore. You can find information on nuclear weapons easily on the internet. Nuclear weapons are composed of elements from basic materials found in nature, such as oxygen, gold, or lead.

Molecules are made up of like elements joined together by electron fields. Compounds are unlike elements joined together by electron fields. Consider an example of water. The molecular structure of water is composed of two elements—two parts hydrogen and one part oxygen. When these two elements are joined, they make water, and are a compound.

An element consists of atoms. Each atom has a nucleus which consists of protons and neutrons.

On a large scale, our solar system's structure is like an atom. The sun is a type of nucleus and the planets (electrons) revolve around it. Why have I explained all of this? Because I believe Peter describes the effect of unleashed nuclear energy.

... in the which the heavens shall pass away with a great noise, and the *elements shall melt with fervent heat*, the earth also and the works that are therein shall be burned up."
—2 Peter 3:10

What is the source of all of this tremendous energy? Simply stated, the atom's nucleus is made up of positively-charged particles called protons. Even though like charges repel, the nucleus stays together. Around the nucleus are a number of orbiting negatively-charged particles, called electrons. The positively-charged nucleus and the negatively-charged electrons are opposite charges and should attract each other. If they did, the atom would collapse. The powerful force that holds the nucleus together, yet keeps the electron field from collapsing is unknown to scientists. They did call it *binding energy* or *residual strong force*, but now scientists call it the *colour force*. But we know what really holds the atom together by reading the Bible.

"For by him were all things created, that are in heaven, and that are in earth, visible and invisible, whether they be thrones, or dominions, or principalities, or powers: all things were created by him, and for him: And he is before all things, *and by him all things consist."* —*Colossians 1:16, 17*

The word *consist* means to *hold together*. Therefore, all things are held together by Him (Jesus). There is a scripture in Hebrews that mentions this power also.

"Who being the brightness of his glory, and the express image of his person, *and upholding all things by the word of his power,* when he had by himself purged our sins, sat down on the right hand of the Majesty on high."—*Hebrews 1:3*

I believe *His Word* is the *binding energy* of the atom.

When nuclear *fission* (the splitting of the atom) occurs, what takes place is very interesting. A stray neutron flies through space, strikes the nucleus of the atom, splits it in two, and forms two new nuclei. One nucleus will always be larger than the other. The difference between the mass of the two new atoms and the original mass of the nucleus is called *mass defect*. Mass defect is composed of heat and energy which, when combined with many such fissions, forms the great fireball we see in a nuclear event. A great ball of heat and fire appears along with a tremendous explosion. The fire and the noise are actually the elements "melting with fervent heat" as it says in 2 Peter 3:10.

To further understand the "elements melting with a fervent heat," let's look at a thermonuclear explosion. A thermonuclear explosion consists of a nuclear device, which is used as a trigger. The nuclear device sits behind a blast shield. When the device is detonated, the blast shield is able to hold back the great heat and pressure for a millisecond.

On the other side of the blast shield is a container made up of a heavy, nonradioactive element. This container holds tritium and other heavy elements. You cannot join these elements together under normal circumstances. If they were combined into an element, it would immediately go into a state of critical mass and fission. Therefore, they are kept separate. When the device is detonated, the great heat and pressure destroys the blast shield and fuses (joins together through great pressure) these elements into one heavy element not naturally found on earth. This element in turn fissions (splits the atoms). This is *thermonuclear fission*. These actions cause the *massive* fireball of the thermonuclear weapon. We actually see the "elements melted with fervent heat" to cause the earth around it to "pass away" as described in 2 Peter 3:10.

Man and his weapons

Man has never made a weapon he didn't intend to use. Many nations enjoy the power and prestige of having their own nuclear arsenal.

In the late sixties and early seventies, a scientist estimated that if the accumulative TNT power of that day were to be divided up, each and every person on the planet earth would get ten thousand pounds delivered to their house. A family of five would receive fifty-thousand pounds of TNT, a total of twenty-five tons. Just the sheer weight alone would crush them all, not to mention its tremendous explosive power. Consider that countries worldwide continued to build nuclear weapons through the seventies, eighties, nineties, and are still building more of them. There are now tens of thousands of nuclear weapons throughout the world. How much explosive power do you suppose could be delivered to everyone's house today?

A ton is two-thousand pounds. Multiply 2,000 by one million and the result is one megaton. A megaton is equal to the explosive power of one million tons of TNT. Each of the tens of thousands of nuclear weapons is equal to at least five megatons in power. This means there are millions of megatons of accumulative TNT power stockpiled—enough nuclear destructive power to destroy the world.

TNT is a shattering, highly explosive compound made up of Trinitrotoluene, which has nitroglycerin as its principle ingredient. To give an example of the explosive power of TNT, if I held an eighth of a pound in my hand and detonated it, I would be blown to pieces by its powerful explosion. The room I was in would be destroyed, windows would be shattered, and the walls would collapse. The explosion tears, shatters, and destroys. This poor forty-ninth generation does not have much to look forward to in light of this knowledge. N

We had a very good saying in bomb disposal school, "When in danger, when in doubt, run in circles, scream and shout." Without the hope of Jesus I think that is an appropriate saying for everyone today.

Destruction and the Thief D

When they say *peace and prosperity*, always remember, sudden destruction will be coming.

When speaking of the Lord's coming, both Paul and Peter combine the phrase, *a thief in the night* with a destructive event.

"But the day of the Lord will come as a *thief in the night*; in the which the heavens shall pass away with a great noise, and the elements shall melt with fervent heat, the earth also and the works that are therein shall be burned up." —*2 Peter 3:10* D

"For yourselves know perfectly that the day of the Lord so cometh as a *thief in the night*. For when they shall say, Peace and safety; then sudden destruction cometh upon them, as travail upon a woman with child; and they shall not escape."—*1 Thessalonians 5:2, 3* D

It seems that Peter, an uneducated fisherman (Acts 4:13), and Paul, who was highly educated, only crossed paths occasionally while on the mission field. Paul wrote that Peter was the apostle to the Jews and that he, Paul, was the apostle to the Gentiles (Galatians 2:8).

Both men had the same vision of the Lord's coming. Peter wrote detailed information about the cataclysmic event, while Paul expanded our view by stating that the event will be preceded by a worldwide delusion of *peace and safety*, which will be followed by sudden destruction.

It is not a coincidence that both Peter and Paul compared "the day of the Lord" with "the thief in the night." God was establishing, through the mouth of two witnesses, the certainty of this event.

Judgment on Gentile Nations

Jeremiah chapter 25 foretells of calamitous events that will come upon the Gentile nations as God prepares to bring the final seven years of judgment upon Israel. N

"For thus saith the LORD God of Israel unto me; Take the wine cup of this fury at my hand, and cause all the nations, to whom I send thee, to drink it. And they shall drink, and be moved, and be mad, because of the sword that I will send among them."—*Jeremiah 25:15, 16*

"Therefore thou shalt say unto them, Thus saith the LORD of hosts, the God of Israel; Drink ye, and be drunken, and spue, and fall, and rise no more, because of the sword which I will send among you. And it shall be, if they refuse to take the cup at thine hand to drink, then shalt thou say unto them, Thus saith the LORD of hosts; Ye shall certainly drink. For, lo, I begin to bring evil on the city which is called by my name, and should ye be utterly unpunished? Ye shall not be unpunished: for I will call for a sword upon all the inhabitants of the earth, saith the LORD of hosts."—*Jeremiah 25:27–29*

"Therefore prophesy thou against them all these words, and say unto them, The LORD shall roar from on high, and utter his voice from his holy habitation; he shall mightily roar upon his habitation; he shall give a shout, as they that tread the grapes, against all the inhabitants of the earth. A noise shall come even to the ends of the earth; for the LORD hath a controversy with the nations, he will plead with all flesh; he will give them that are wicked to the sword, saith the LORD. Thus saith the LORD of hosts, Behold, evil shall go forth from nation to nation, and a great whirlwind shall be raised up from the coasts of the earth. And the slain of the LORD shall be at that day from one end of the earth even unto the other end of the earth: they shall not be lamented, neither gathered, nor buried; they shall be dung upon the ground."
—*Jeremiah 25:30–33*

Careless living

In Ezekiel chapter 39, scripture says that as the nations retreat from Israel, fire rains from the sky upon them. This fire rains upon those Gentiles that live carelessly in the isles, and upon Gog and Magog.

"And I will send a fire on Magog, and among *them that dwell carelessly in the isles*: and they shall know that I am the LORD."—*Ezekiel 39:6*

"Then the five men departed, and came to Laish, and saw the people that were therein, *how they dwelt careless*, after the manner of the Zidonians, quiet and secure; and there was no magistrate in the land, that might put them to shame in any thing; and they were far from the Zidonians, and had no business with any man."—*Judges 18:7*

Careless living spoken of in Judges 18:7 means to *create a lifestyle that eliminates shame and guilt*. Today's progressives claim that a society free of shame and guilt is their ultimate goal.

Recently, *The American Chronicle printed an* article which said that the deepest fear of progressives "is that the United States would become a theocracy where a religion (in their view, a fundamentalist Christian religion), would be imposed on the country. This theocracy would subsequently eliminate gays and impose various other restrictions on the guilt-free lifestyles that progressives live and advocate[†]."

I hope you get the drift about the move towards careless living and the accompanying consequences coming to this generation. The book of Jeremiah tells what will happen to those who have lived carelessly.

"And the slain of the LORD shall be at that day from one end of the earth even unto the other end of the earth: they shall not be lamented,

[†]This article can be viewed in its entirety at: http://www.inthedays.com/hated-for-his-names-sake/the-religious-right-hurts-america. Source: http://www.americanchronicle.com/articles/viewArticle.asp?articleID=17160

neither gathered, nor buried; they shall be dung upon the ground."—*Jeremiah 25:33*

It's time to look up

The words Jesus spoke as recorded in the Gospel of Luke take on deeper meaning.

"And when these things begin to come to pass, then *look up*, and lift up your heads; for your redemption draweth nigh."—*Luke 21:28* W

Remember, I theorize that the "day of the Lord" is the Redeemer coming for His purchased possession and at the same time the beginning of judgment on both Jews and Gentiles.

As I thought about this scenario, I considered, "Who would miss us if we were raptured? If there was no one to bury the dead or mourn for the dead all over the earth, who will miss us?"

No one will even understand. There will be utter chaos.

"For *the Lord himself* shall descend from heaven with a shout, with the voice of the archangel, and with the trump of God: and the dead in Christ shall rise first: Then *we which are alive and remain* shall be caught up together with them in the clouds, to meet the Lord in the air: and so shall we ever be with the Lord."—*1 Thessalonians 4:16, 17*

Chapter 9: Deliverance

At the end of the last chapter, I introduced the word *rapture*. In this chapter, we will look more closely at its meaning and the teaching (doctrine) that surrounds it. Also mentioned was the deliverance of the righteous from God's judgment and the redemption of the purchased possession (Ephesians 1:14). *Rapture* is a single word that describes this entire event. It is not a new doctrine. R W

I want to illustrate the actual event to illuminate the state of happiness we will encounter as we meet the Lord when He redeems and delivers us from this evil world.

Entering into God's presence is such a wonderful hope that all the church should be anticipating it with pleasure. The early church believed in this teaching and held fast to the hope that it produced in their lives.

Hope rejected

Today, sad to say, we see the other extreme. Some people believe that the doctrine of the rapture is something that the church created in the nineteenth and twentieth centuries. Yet this teaching is as old as the New Testament.

Over the centuries the teaching of the rapture was shelved as the traditions of the church replaced the teaching of God's Word. However, as the Holy Spirit revived the church with the Reformation movement, believers gained the freedom to read the Word of God, and the doctrine of the coming of the Lord for His church revived.

This took place slowly, for the Word had to be translated into the common language of that day and then be printed and distributed to the people. This was resisted by the established church.

After it was distributed, the Word was studied by called men and women of God. The Reformation began about 1515–1520, and William Tyndale's English translation of the Bible was first published in 1526. As the Bible was slowly distributed, people gained knowledge of the truth.

In the middle of the nineteenth century, John Nelson Darby (1800–1882) from England, used the Hebrew and the Greek of a previous translation to translate the scriptures. Darby is known as the father of modern *dispensationalism*, a belief in a system of historical progression believed to be revealed in the Bible, consisting of a series of stages in God's self-revelation plan of salvation.

During his studies of this concept, John Darby is credited for the rediscovery of the doctrine of the catching away of the church (rapture). Whether or not one believes in the dispensational doctrine isn't the point to be discussed here. What demands our examination is the teaching of the rapture. The doctrine was dormant from Darby's time until it gained great popularity in the revival of the late 1960s, continuing strong until the mid-1980s.

New found purification

In 1988, a prophecy came to our church—that by 1992, the soon coming of Jesus Christ for His church would again become a diminished doctrine and looked upon as a bizarre teaching. At this writing, in many sectors both secular and Christian, the *rapture* is believed to be a cultish doctrine or a quirky teaching. Because this doctrine is so scriptural, I still believe it, preach it, and hold fast to it.

In fact, I believe that the rapture of the church (redemption), the *carrying of the church into heaven as deliverance from judgment,* is a supremely important teaching. Because this subject is frequently argued over among believers, it is often neglected from the pulpit. Yet scripture promises teaching this doctrine will bring a very *purifying result* on the believer. R W

"Beloved, now are we the sons of God, and it doth not yet appear what we shall be: but we know that, when he shall appear, we shall be like him; for we shall see him as he is. And every man that hath this hope in him purifieth himself, even as he is pure."—*1 John 3:2–3*

Happy Church

The scripture also clearly states the blessed hope of the church is the coming of the Lord.

"Looking for *that blessed hope*, and the glorious appearing of the great God and our Saviour Jesus Christ."—*Titus 2:13*

The word *hope* means to *anticipate with pleasure and confident assurance*. The word *blessed* means *happy*. So I am *happily anticipating with pleasure and confidence* the coming of Jesus Christ. This is a hope that should never be taken away from the church. The fact that the rapture could come at any moment should cause the church to be alive!

Heartsick Church

Proverbs speaks of hope.

"Hope deferred maketh the heart sick: but when the desire cometh, it is a tree of life." —*Proverbs 13:12*

People place themselves in danger when they say the Lord is delaying his coming (Luke 12:45).

Some Bible teachers have placed Jesus' coming for the church at the end of the tribulation, while others have taught that it happens at the end of the thousand years (see *Chapter 11: With All His Saints*, first paragraph). Some even teach that Jesus will not come until the world is under the dominion of the church.

Teachers who expound these views are probably driven by the love of money and power instead of the scriptural "blessed hope." The things of the world, church pressures, and our great plans all must take second place to the coming of the Lord. These teachings result in "hope deferred" and thereby cause many Christians to be heartsick.

Our happiness is provable

My belief is that the Bible proves the pre-tribulation rapture. If you read the Bible from the beginning to end, you will discover when the Gentile church started to grow and when it will be harvested. W

Peter, speaking of this time of harvest (redemption, or deliverance), said that the Lord knows how to deliver the righteous from judgment. He used the examples of Noah and Lot to emphasize the point.

"And spared not the old world, *but saved Noah* the eighth person, a preacher of righteousness, bringing in the flood upon the world of the ungodly; And turning the cities of Sodom and Gomorrha into ashes condemned them with an overthrow, making them an ensample unto those that after should live ungodly; *And delivered just Lot*, vexed with the filthy conversation of the wicked: (For that righteous man dwelling among them, in seeing and hearing, vexed his righteous soul from day to day with their unlawful deeds;) *The Lord knoweth how to deliver the godly* out of temptations, and to reserve the unjust unto the day of judgment to be punished." *—2 Peter 2:5–9*

Jesus said that as His Second Coming approached, life on this planet would take on the attributes of the days of Noah and Lot (Luke 17:26–32). In *Chapter 8: The Last Generation*, we examined those passages in reference to the signs of the times. Now, we will use scripture to examine the deliverance of the righteous before judgment. Judgment did not come until Noah entered the Ark.

"And every living substance was destroyed which was upon the face of the ground, both man, and cattle, and the creeping things, and the fowl of the heaven; and they were destroyed from the earth: and Noah only remained alive, and they that were with him in the ark."*—Genesis 7:23*

In Lot's case, judgment was withheld until Lot and his family were led to safety by angels.

"...I will not overthrow this city, for the which thou hast spoken. Haste thee, escape thither; for I cannot do any thing till thou be come thither..."*—Genesis 19:21, 22*

"But the same day that Lot went out of Sodom it rained fire and brimstone from heaven, and destroyed them all."*—Luke 17:29*

The scriptures teach that the church will be delivered from the wrath of God, by being *caught up* (raptured) to meet Jesus Christ in the air. Belief in this teaching causes action on the part of the believer.

Let's say you believed the rapture was coming tonight. What would you do? Would you find people to tell and risk being called a religious fanatic? That's what Lot did, even though he was ridiculed by his own family.

"And Lot went out, and spake unto his sons in law, which married his daughters, and said, Up, get you out of this place; for the LORD will destroy this city. But he seemed as one that mocked unto his sons in law."*—Genesis 19:14*

If you knew that the rapture was imminent, would you be compelled to tell people about Jesus Christ, or would you continue as a secret Christian? I think you'd be really excited; you might even change your lifestyle. You see, the rapture is a life-changing doctrine—it *refocuses* your life!

The Diligent Watchers

Let's move on in our deeper look at this subject. The New Testament book of 1 Thessalonians clearly shows that the

Thessalonian people were diligently waiting for Jesus Christ to come again.

"For they themselves shew of us what manner of entering in we had unto you, and how ye *turned to God from idols* to serve the living and true God; *And to wait for his Son from heaven*, whom he raised from the dead, *even Jesus, which delivered us from the wrath to come."* —*1 Thessalonians 1:9, 10*

It's important to note that when 1 Thessalonians was written, Christianity had just begun. Previous to this letter, Paul had come to their city and preached Jesus Christ crucified. He had taught them that if they would accept Jesus as God's sacrifice for sins, they would be born again and have eternal life.

The Greek Thessalonians did not know about Abraham, Isaac, Jacob, the promised land, or Jesus Christ prior to Paul's visit. They had no conscious knowledge of Noah and the flood or Adam and Eve. Through ignorance, the Thessalonians worshipped many pagan idols such as the goddess Diana, a multifaceted idol and mother of many children. Other gods they worshipped included Zeus, the chief god, and Neptune, their god of the underworld.

New insights

As people in Thessalonica accepted this message of Jesus, they turned from these false gods and started waiting for the Second Coming of Christ and deliverance from the wrath to come.

However, a problem arose. As time passed some of their numbers died. They still expected the Lord to return at any moment, but they were ignorant concerning the state of their departed loved ones and were sorrowing without hope as do unbelievers. To this anxious people Paul wrote these encouraging words.

"To the end he may stablish your hearts unblameable in holiness before God, even our Father, at the coming of our Lord Jesus Christ *with all his saints."—1 Thessalonians 3:13*

Here, the Thessalonians were informed that when Jesus did come from heaven, all His *saints* would accompany Him. In the light of the problem Paul was addressing, I am sure that the Thessalonians knew very well the meaning of the word *saint.* However, the word *saint* these days brings different images to peoples' minds. Let's take a detour and scripturally define the word *saint.*

What does *Saint* mean?

The Word of God points out that we are all *saints* if we have accepted the Lord Jesus Christ as our Saviour. Yet many have been taught by the church that this title only belongs to someone that has never sinned and has been Canonized. In reality, though, saint is defined as *a sinner saved by Grace.* The epistles are addressed to *the saints*—that is, to *believers.*

"To all that be in Rome, beloved of God, called *to be saints*: Grace to you and peace from God our Father, and the Lord Jesus Christ." —*Romans 1:7*

"Unto the church of God which is at Corinth, to them that are sanctified in Christ Jesus, called *to be saints*, with all that in every place call upon the name of Jesus Christ our Lord, both theirs and ours."—*1 Corinthians 1:2*

In both verses, *to be* has been inserted by the translators. It really reads, *to them that are sanctified in Christ Jesus, called saints.* Called means *invited* and saints implies *virtuous.* I believe the word *saint* embodies all the attributes of a sanctified person. This sanctification comes to the believer through the work of Jesus Himself.

"…we are sanctified through the offering of the body of Jesus Christ once for all." —*Hebrews 10:10*

The Greek word for sanctified is *hagiazo,* and comes from the word translated *saint* in English. Therefore, saint could be short for *sanctified by Jesus.*

These verses in Revelation give further insight as to the identity of saints.

"He that overcometh, the same shall be clothed in white raiment; and I will not blot out his name out of the book of life, but I will confess his name before my Father, and before his angels."—*Revelation 3:5*

"And to her was granted that she should be arrayed in fine linen, clean and white: for the fine linen is the righteousness of saints." —*Revelation 19:8*

White raiment is the clothing of overcomers in Revelation 3:5, and white linen is the "righteousness of the saints" in Revelation 19:8, making overcomers and saints synonymous. How do we overcome? By the finished work of Jesus.

What about those who have died?

As we move on in the letter Paul continues to deal with the issue of their departed loved ones.

"But I *would not have you to be ignorant,* brethren, concerning them which are *asleep,* that ye sorrow not, even as others which have no hope."—*1 Thessalonians 4:13*

The Greek word for *ignorant* in this verse basically means *not to understand.* Therefore, the Lord wanted all to understand the mystery of His Coming for the church.

The Greek word for *asleep* in this verse means *died.* The same word is used for *fell asleep* in the story of Stephen in the book of Acts. Stephen preached the Gospel to the Sanhedrin. At the end of Stephen's message he rebuked and confronted them.

"Ye stiffnecked and uncircumcised in heart and ears, ye do always resist the Holy Ghost: as your fathers did, so do ye. Which of the prophets have not your fathers persecuted? and they have slain them which shewed before of the coming of the Just One; of whom ye have been now the betrayers and murderers." —*Acts 7:51, 52*

Upon hearing this rebuke, they dragged him out of the city and stoned him to death.

"And they stoned Stephen, calling upon God, and saying, Lord Jesus, receive my spirit. And he kneeled down, and cried with a loud voice, Lord, lay not this sin to their charge. And when he had said this, *he fell asleep.*"—*Acts 7:59, 60*

Just by reading this scripture, you can see that Stephen didn't take a nap. In the world's eyes, he *died.* As Stephen looked up to heaven and saw Jesus, a peace came upon him that prompted him to ask God not to charge this deed to their account. (The Greek words for asleep are the same in both cases.) I'm sure that Paul had that event in mind when he wrote by the Holy Spirit about the death of believers in 2 Corinthians.

"Therefore we are always confident, knowing that, whilst we are at home in the body, we are absent from the Lord: (For we walk by faith, not by sight.)"—*2 Corinthians 5:6, 7*

Reflected Light

Scripture tells us about this change.

"...we shall all be changed, in a moment, in the twinkling of an eye, at the last trump: for the trumpet shall sound, and the dead shall be raised incorruptible, and we shall be changed. For this corruptible must put on incorruption, and this mortal must put on immortality."
—*1 Corinthians 15:51–53*

Your eye twinkles because it reflects light. Light travels at the speed of 186,000 miles per second, or 669,600,000 miles per hour. This is the speed at which things move during the transition between mortality and immortality. If it were possible to be at the equator and travel at the speed of light, you could travel around the earth 7-3/4 times in one second.

This quick transition from life to eternal life, takes place at the moment of your death or the rapture of the Church, whichever comes first. And so we will forever be with the Lord.

We don't have to mourn

In the light of these facts, the statement Paul made concerning those who are asleep takes on new, personal meaning.

"...concerning them which are asleep, that ye sorrow not, even as others which have no hope."—*1 Thessalonians 4:13*

Have you lost a relative or someone close? Did they know the Lord Jesus Christ as their Saviour? If the answers to these questions are yes, then know for sure you don't have to mourn for them. For they are not in the grave waiting for the Lord, or suspended in some kind of purgatory or soul-sleep. They are in His presence. When they died, they left their earthly bodies behind and at the speed of light entered into the presence of God. Paul continues to encourage the church.

"For if we believe that Jesus died and rose again, even so *them also which sleep in Jesus will God bring with him*."—*1 Thessalonians 4:14*

More to believe

The Thessalonians surely believed that "Jesus died and rose again" for they had been watching for Him to return. But now they were given more to believe, "Them also which sleep in Jesus will God bring with him."

Now the Thessalonians could put the facts together and conclude that the saints mentioned as returning with Jesus in 1 Thessalonians chapter 3, and the ones that sleep in Him are the same—more proof that a saint is simply a believer.

I'm sure this information brought comfort to the Thessalonians. It should also bring comfort to us, for through this we know exactly what happened to our believing loved ones when they left this world.

Absent from the body, present with the Lord

I have seen illustrated Bible tracts depicting the rapture. As the rapture takes place in these illustrations, the graves open up and ghostly images ascend upward as if going to heaven. Great cartoons—but that's not how it's going to happen. Believers are not in the graves, they are present with the Lord in their Heavenly bodies and are coming back with Him. Paul wrote and assured us of this, and follows with his conclusion.

"We are confident, I say, and willing rather to be absent from the body, and to be present with the Lord."—*2 Corinthians 5:8*

Good-bye old body—Hello new body!
Paul didn't say absent from the body is to be in the grave. Through these scriptures, we can clearly understand that a believer who dies in Christ is instantly in His presence.

"For we know that if our earthly house of this tabernacle were dissolved, we have a building of God, an house not made with hands, eternal in the heavens. *For in this we groan, earnestly desiring to be clothed upon with our house* which is from heaven: If so be that being clothed *we shall not be found naked.* For we that are in this tabernacle do groan, being burdened: *not for that we would be unclothed, but clothed upon,* that mortality might be swallowed up of life."—*2 Corinthians 5: 1–4*

Unclothed means to be without a body. Waiting in a grave for any length of time would lead to decomposition, leaving you *unclothed*, negating 2 Corinthians 5:4.

This hope we have before us to be with the Lord is not deferred. Therefore, when my time comes I'll be saying, "Good-bye earthly body, hello heavenly body," and I will have access to the Tree of Life.

Spiritual order
Paul assures the Thessalonians with the spiritual order of events. He states that their loved ones who were already *asleep* would not be held back from being with the Lord.

"For this we say unto you by the word of the Lord, that we which are alive and remain unto the coming of the Lord shall not *prevent* them which are asleep."—*1 Thessalonians 4:15*

He simply stated that those that sleep in Christ do not have to wait for the coming of the Son from heaven in order to be in God's presence. In the next verses Paul goes on to reveal more of this fantastic mystery.

"For t*he Lord himself* shall descend from heaven with a shout, with the voice of the archangel, and with the trump of God: and the dead in Christ shall rise first: Then *we which are alive and remain* shall be caught up together with them in the clouds, to meet the Lord in the air: and so shall we ever be with the Lord."
—*1 Thessalonians 4:16, 17*

Simple logic
Now, let's put this all together. Paul states that when a believer dies, he is immediately with the Lord (2 Corinthians 5:8).

In 1 Thessalonians 4:16 and 17, Paul wrote about the saints meeting Jesus at His coming. He established that all of His saints would meet together with Him in the air.

A colon is used to introduce a clause explaining the phrase that precedes it. Notice the colon at the end of 1 Thessalonians 4:16 preceding *v*erse 17 which begins, "Then *we which are alive and remain* shall be caught up together with them in the clouds…" Paul stated that the Lord would "descend from heaven with the voice of the angel and the trump of God," and Paul expands the thought with the fact that before this, the dead are already with the Lord and will return with Him. Because of the colon, the phrase at the end of 1 Thessalonians 4:16, "the dead in Christ shall rise first:" means "the dead in Christ have already risen."

Paul is saying that the saints that had died couldn't come back with the Lord to meet the living saints in the air unless they were with Him prior to His coming.

I believe the Day of the Lord will be a very personal day for everyone. For on that wonderful day, Jesus will come with the voice of an archangel and will simultaneously call out the name of His living followers. Consider when Jesus went to Lazarus' tomb.

"And when he thus had spoken, he cried with a loud voice, Lazarus, come forth."—*John 11:43*

Jesus called Lazarus personally by name. Had Jesus merely said, "Come forth," all the dead would have risen. I believe that if He shouts, "Come up hither," all the people on the earth will go up. Therefore, Jesus is going to be so personal with us that He will call each of us by name, and leave behind those who have rejected the Gospel of Salvation.

Why was Lazarus in the grave and not present with the Lord? Prior to the death of Jesus Christ for the sins of the world, access to the Father and heaven was unobtainable. Jesus mentioned this fact in Luke when He told the story of the beggar and the rich man.

"And it came to pass, that the beggar died, and was carried by the angels into Abraham's bosom: the rich man also died, and was buried."—*Luke 16:22*

Abraham's bosom was the place of the righteous dead prior to the death of Jesus. The beggar was *asleep* in Abraham's bosom until the day came that Jesus' death paid for the sins of the world. Then Jesus emptied Abraham's bosom and took *captivity* captive.

"Wherefore he saith, When he ascended up on high, he led *captivity captive*, and gave gifts unto men."—*Ephesians 4:8*

"And the graves were opened; and many bodies of the saints which slept arose, And came out of the graves after his resurrection, and went into the holy city, and appeared unto many." —*Matthew 27:52, 53*

If there were such a thing as *soul sleep*, Abraham's place would still be full.

"Wherefore comfort one another with these words."—*1 Thessalonians 4:18*

We can be comforted when we lose someone here on this earth who knew the Lord. We cry and mourn, and yes, we should—after all we have suffered a loss. However, there is no need to mourn for the ones who have died, they are really happy. We mourn for the living who have lost, temporarily, their loved ones.

More about the Rapture to come

I have only touched on the basics of the doctrine of the rapture, but there is still time to be part of the greatest family reunion of all time. To me it is very exciting to know that when He comes for His church, I'm going to be reunited with all my regenerated family that have gone before me. It's also exciting to realize that He is coming for living people and that He's not waiting for every believer to die before He judges the world!

"Sing unto the LORD with the harp; with the harp, and the voice of a psalm. With trumpets and sound of cornet make a joyful noise before the LORD, the King. Let the sea roar, and the fulness thereof; the world, and they that dwell therein. Let the floods clap their hands: let the hills be joyful together Before the LORD; for he cometh to judge the earth: with righteousness shall he judge the world, and the people with equity."—*Psalm 98: 5–9*

Chapter 10: The Order Of Things

In Paul's second letter to the Thessalonian people, he established the events on earth that would precede this great family reunion.

"Now we beseech you, brethren, by the coming of our Lord Jesus Christ, and by our gathering together unto him, That ye be not soon shaken in mind, or be troubled, neither by spirit, nor by word, nor by letter as from us, as that the day of Christ is at hand. Let no man deceive you by any means: for that day shall not come, except there come a *falling away first*, and that man of sin be revealed, the son of perdition."
—*2 Thessalonians 2:1–3*

Great Falling Away

In this verse, the words *falling away* are actually the English rendering for the Greek word *apostasia* (ap-os-tas-ee'-ah). This word is defined in Strong's Bible Concordance as: *defection from truth, falling away or forsaking*. We find *apostasia* translated as *forsake* in Acts.

"And they are informed of thee, that thou teachest all the Jews which are among the Gentiles to *forsake* Moses, saying that they ought not to circumcise their children, neither to walk after the customs."—*Acts 21:21*

Therefore, in 2 Thessalonians the *falling away* could also be interpreted as *the forsaking or defection of the faith by the church*. This sounds like the lukewarm Laodicean church in Revelation. However, there is another way to look at this word.

Two necessary events

Second Thessalonians 2:3 sheds some more light on the definition of the word *apostasia*. As previously stated, Paul said there would first need to be a *falling away* (a forsaking first), and then *that man of sin be revealed, the son of perdition*.

Therefore, two things have to happen before Christ can return. One would be the *departure, or defection from the truth,* and the other, *that the man of sin be revealed*. More light is shed on this mystery in the same chapter.

"For the mystery of iniquity doth already work: only he who now *letteth* will let, until he be taken out of the way. And then shall *that Wicked* be revealed, whom the Lord shall consume with the spirit of his mouth, and shall destroy with the brightness of his coming."
—*2 Thessalonians 2:7, 8*

The withholding force

The word *letteth* in the Greek language is *katecho* (kat-ekh'-o): *to hold down, possess, retain, seize on, stay, take, withhold*. Therefore, whatever is *taken out of the way* is something that is *retaining or withholding*. What really impresses me about this verse is that it points out "that Wicked" won't be revealed until something is removed. It seems to me the Thessalonians knew what this restraining force was.

"And now ye know what *withholdeth* that he might be revealed in his time." —*2 Thessalonians 2:6*

The Removal

I believe that the Thessalonian people were assured that the church was, and still is, the retaining, or *withholding* force that prevents iniquity from coming to its fullness in the world. The church must be removed from this position for the scriptures to be fulfilled.

This removal could happen in one of two ways. The church could simply become involved with this world, no longer holding to the doctrines of Christ. Or, it could continue to serve the Lord in obedience to the faith, holding itself separate from the world until the day of the rapture.

If the church forsakes the truth and becomes lukewarm, then it would be true that the church would no longer be withholding iniquity. But this would bring the faithful remnant of the church under "the wrath to come" with the rest of the unbelieving world. Would the people in Thessalonians and Hebrews be spiritually alive and looking for the Lord when He comes if they had departed from the faith? The Thessalonians were waiting not only for the coming of Jesus, but also for deliverance from the wrath to come. W

Watchers and Withholders

As Jesus descends from heaven, this group of followers will be "caught up" to meet Him in the air.

"Then we which are alive and remain shall be *caught up* together with them in the clouds, to meet the Lord in the air: and so shall we ever be with the Lord."—*1 Thessalonians 4:17*

"So Christ was once offered to bear the sins of many; and unto them that look for him shall he appear the second time without sin unto salvation."—*Hebrews 9:28*

These scriptures tell me that it's definitely not going to be an unbelieving church to which Jesus Christ will come before the Antichrist is revealed. He will come to a world where a group of followers are watching and waiting for Him. Because these believers are watching and not lukewarm, something is withholding iniquity from coming to its fullness. Therefore, the watchers and the withholders are one and the same. So the "*falling away*" in 2 Thessalonians 2:3 and the removal of the *retaining force* in 2 Thessalonians 2:7 are one and the same.

The Church—The Withholder

The church today is comprised of true believers and defectors from the truth. The true believers are the restraining force in the world. When the true believers are raptured, all that will be left are the defectors. Today, we see the beginning of the falling away of the church, but after the rapture, the defection will become rampant. When that happens, all iniquity will break loose. Men's hearts will be continuously wicked, and the transgressors on the planet assume unrestrained control.

Daniel was told that in the latter times, there would be a dominance of Greek philosophy (democracy). During this time, the transgressors would come to the full, and the wicked one would come to power.

"And in the latter time of their kingdom, when the transgressors are come to the full, a king of fierce countenance, and understanding dark sentences, shall stand up."—*Daniel 8:23*

The force that carries away

Another bit of light that reinforces this belief is found in the Greek word *harpazo*. In the Strong's Bible Concordance *harpazo* (har-pad'-zo) means; *to catch (away, up) pluck, pull, take (by force)*. Harpazo can be read as *to carry away by force, to claim for one's self eagerly*, and *to be snatched away*. Let's examine a few instances of how this word is used in the scriptures, beginning with Matthew.

"When any one heareth the word of the kingdom, and understandeth it not, then cometh the wicked one, and *catcheth away* that which was sown in his heart. This is he which received seed by the way side."—*Matthew 13:19*

Here *harpazo* is translated into the phrase "catcheth away" which depicts the *taking of something away, spiritually*. It is used by Jesus to illustrate the safety of the believer.

"And I give unto them eternal life; and they shall never perish, neither shall any man *pluck* them out of my hand."—*John 10:28*

In John 10:28, *Harpazo* is translated as *pluck*. So no one will be able to *snatch* you out of the hand of Jesus Christ. Now let's return to the passage that we started with.

"For the Lord himself shall descend from heaven with a shout, with the voice of the archangel, and with the trump of God: and the dead in Christ shall rise first: Then we which are alive and remain shall be *caught up* together with them in the clouds, to meet the Lord in the air: and so shall we ever be with the Lord. Wherefore comfort one another with these words."—*1 Thessalonians 4:16–18*

Harpazo and *caught up* are one and the same. Another very interesting use for *harpazo* is found in Acts.

"And when they were come up out of the water, the Spirit of the Lord *caught away* Philip, that the eunuch saw him no more: and he went on his way rejoicing."—*Acts 8:39*

The words *caught away*, again, is the word *harpazo*. Philip was *harpazoed* and the eunuch saw him no more. Philip then found himself in another city.

"But Philip was found at Azotus: and passing through he preached in all the cities, till he came to Caesarea."—*Acts 8:40*

So Philip was *translated*—he was *caught up, raptured*. In another scripture Paul uses this word to describe his being brought into the heavens by God.

"I knew a man in Christ above fourteen years ago, (whether in the body, I cannot tell; or whether out of the body, I cannot tell: God knoweth;) such an one *caught up* to the third heaven."—*2 Corinthians 12:2*

Finally, the Greek word *harpazo* is translated *rapturous* (or *raptus*) in Latin. Therefore the Latin form of *harpazo* is the basis for our English word *rapture*.

Two witnesses

As a result of the rapture of the church, the earth will be void of the witness of the finished work of Jesus during the seven years of God's judgment. But God will not leave that forsaken society without an opportunity to hear the truth and repent. God will provide two powerful witnesses during this time. And the spirit of grace will now come upon Israel and the testimony of Jesus will be accomplished by the Jewish people themselves.

These two prophets, the "two witnesses," are found in Revelation chapter 11. Their ministry, based in Jerusalem, will last for three and one-half years. N

"And I will give power unto my two witnesses, and they shall prophesy a thousand two hundred and threescore days, clothed in sackcloth."—*Revelation 11:3*

I believe their ministry will be used to bring the 144,000 Jews to Jesus (Revelation chapter 7). These 144,000 Jews will join with the two witnesses. God eventually allows the Antichrist to kill the two witnesses, leaving their bodies in public view for three and one-half days (Revelation 11:7–9).

At the end of this time, the Spirit of the Lord comes upon them and they rise from the dead in full public view. The two witnesses and the 144,000 sealed Jewish servants are taken into heaven. Angels are given the assignment of preaching to the world for the last three and one-half years of tribulation.

A sad world

At this point in the tribulation all Jewish and Gentile believers have ascended into heaven. Sad to say, this leaves us with another group—those who rejected Jesus Christ. Their destiny is *Hell.*

Hell is not the place depicted in the movies or television. Scripturally, it is actually two places known as *Hades* and *Gehenna. Hades* is a compartment some place in the earth that is evidently hot and dry, where the rejectors of salvation are waiting and will wait for the Great White Throne Judgment.

There is no hope for those that have rejected Jesus Christ. There is no second chance. They are brought up from Hades at the end of the Millennium for judgment at the Great White Throne. After judgment, they are sent to their final and permanent dwelling place of the lost known as *Gehenna. Hades* is called hell; *Gehenna* is called the *Lake of Fire* (Revelation 20:11–15).

Jesus Himself referred to *Gehenna* eleven times. *Gehenna* is the place that was originally prepared for Satan and his angels, not mankind.

"Then shall he say also unto them on the left hand, Depart from me, ye cursed, into everlasting fire, *prepared for the devil and his angels."—Matthew 25:41*

People are not sent there by God. People go to everlasting fire prepared for the devil and his angels because they have rejected Jesus Christ and chosen to follow Satan. The only reason people wind up there is because their names are not written in the *Lamb's Book of Life.*

"And whosoever was not found written in the book of life was cast into the lake of fire."
—*Revelation 20:15*

"When the Lord shall build up Zion, he shall appear in his glory."—Psalm 102:16

Chapter 11: With All His Saints

Another interesting subject that pertains to the raptured Church is the future age of the Millennium.

Millennium: "a span of one thousand years; a thousand-year period of holiness mentioned in Revelation 20, during which Jesus and his faithful followers are to rule on earth; a hoped-for period of joy, serenity, prosperity, and justice."—from the *American Heritage Dictionary* U

Here comes the Judge

The *Millennium* begins with the Second Coming of Jesus Christ, as illustrated in Revelation.

"And I saw heaven opened, and behold a white horse; and he that sat upon him was called Faithful and True, and in righteousness he doth judge and make war."—*Revelation 19:11*

Earlier in the New Testament, the scriptures pointed out that Jesus is the one who will come and judge the world.

"Because he hath appointed a day, in the which he will judge the world in righteousness by that man whom he hath ordained; whereof he hath given assurance unto all men, in that he hath raised him from the dead."—*Acts 17:31*

This judgment takes place between Revelation 6:1 and Revelation 19:11 Judgment begins with the first seal.

"And I saw when the Lamb opened one of the seals, and I heard, as it were the noise of thunder, one of the four beasts saying, Come and see."—*Revelation 6:1*

Jesus returns at the last battle of the judgment.

"And I saw heaven opened, and behold a white horse; and he that sat upon him was called Faithful and True, and in righteousness he doth judge and make war. His eyes were as a flame of fire, and on his head were many crowns; and he had a name written, that no man knew, but he himself. And he was clothed with a vesture dipped in blood: and his name is called The Word of God."—*Revelation 19:12, 13*

Judgment begins when Jesus takes the book from Him on the throne and begins to open the seals. In my opinion, this is the beginning of the wrath of God on the world. This will all end with the Second Coming of the Lord Jesus with the clouds of heaven. At that time, every eye shall see Him and every tongue shall wail. T

"Behold, he cometh with clouds; and every eye shall see him, and they also which pierced him: and all kindreds of the earth shall wail because of him. Even so, Amen."—*Revelation 1:7*

Remember, when Jesus first comes as a thief in the night, it is to redeem His saints at the rapture. But at His Second Coming, He will be visible to all of the inhabitants of the earth, and will end the Tribulation judgment. T W

At His return on the white horse, He is identified as the Word of God. The scriptures plainly tell us who the Word of God is.

"In the beginning was the Word, and the Word was with God, and the Word was God." —*John 1:1*

"And the Word was made flesh, and dwelt among us, (and we beheld his glory, the glory as of the only begotten of the Father) full of grace and truth."—*John 1:14*

Through these scriptures, I conclude that the one on the horse in Revelation 19:11 is Jesus Christ. At His first advent, He came as the *Lamb*. He will come at the rapture as the *Redeemer*. At His Second Coming, He will come as the *Judge*. E T

Shadows of Heaven

Earlier in this book, we spoke of the Feast of Tabernacles. Now let's again examine that information and fit it into the period between Revelation chapters 6 and 19.

In the book of Leviticus, Israel celebrated the Feast of Tabernacles after the Day of Atonement.

"And ye shall keep it a feast unto the LORD seven days in the year. It shall be a statute for ever in your generations: ye shall celebrate it in the seventh month. Ye shall dwell in booths seven days; all that are Israelites born shall dwell in booths."—*Leviticus 23:41–42*

I theorize that the Feast of Tabernacles is a foreshadow of the church in heaven during the seven years of tribulation. During the Feast of Tabernacles, which took place after the harvest, the Jews were to leave all their earthly possessions in their houses and move into tents. Each morning they arose, went out and picked up *palm and goodly branches and waved them before the Lord*, for the harvest was over (Leviticus 23:40). Everyday was a Sabbath, a day of rest. As I read the scriptures concerning this ceremony, I understand the body of Christ (believers) to be resting in Heaven while the seven years of tribulation takes place on earth. S N

The group of people who are wearing white robes in Revelation chapter 7, are the ones who came out of the Great Tribulation. They didn't go *through* the Great Tribulation, but came *out* of it. They are identified by their white robes (the righteousness of the saints), as they wave *palm branches* before God in heaven.

"After this I beheld, and, lo, a great multitude, which no man could number, of all nations, and kindreds, and people, and tongues, stood before the throne, and before the Lamb, clothed with white robes, and *palms in their hands*; And cried with a loud voice, saying, Salvation to our God which sitteth upon the throne, and unto the Lamb."—*Revelation 7:9–10*

We all get a flying white horse

As we see Jesus coming back to the earth riding on a white horse, we also see the armies of heaven with Him. T

"And the armies which were in heaven followed him upon white horses, clothed in fine linen, white and clean."—*Revelation 19:14*

Let's identify the armies. Their *white* clothing gives them away.

"And to her was granted that she should be arrayed in fine linen, clean and white: for the fine linen is the righteousness of saints."
—*Revelation 19:8*

The armies are His saints! This makes sense because they are the ones coming back with Jesus. Their *white* clothing also gives them away in Revelation 3:5, where the overcoming church is promised *white* garments. In Revelation 7:14, the saints' robes have been washed clean and made *white* in the blood of the Lamb.

An important distinction

In 1 Thessalonians 3:13, *all* of the saints are prophetically seen returning with Jesus.

"To the end he may stablish your hearts unblameable in holiness before God, even our Father, *at the coming of our Lord Jesus Christ with all his saints*."—*1 Thessalonians 3:13*

In contrast, 1 Thessalonians 4:14 tells us that He brings *only* the saints who have died with Him when He comes for the living saints.

"...them also which sleep in Jesus will God bring with him."—*1 Thessalonians 4:14*

In 1 Thessalonians chapter 4, Paul is not referring to Jesus as the Judge that will make war. Paul is talking about Jesus the Redeemer, coming for those who await redemption and are *alive and watching*—His saints! S W

Two roles—One Saviour

Jesus coming as Redeemer and Jesus coming as Judge are two distinctive events. As stated earlier, Jesus first has to redeem the ones that are alive in order for the redeemed to return with Him when He comes as the Judge.

First, Jesus comes in the air as Redeemer for the Redemption of His saints. R S W

"In whom ye also trusted, after that ye heard the word of truth, the gospel of your salvation: in whom also after that ye believed, ye were sealed with that holy Spirit of promise, Which is the earnest of our inheritance *until the redemption* of the purchased possession, unto the praise of his glory."—*Ephesians 1:13, 14*

"And grieve not the holy Spirit of God, whereby ye are sealed *unto the day of redemption*."
—*Ephesians 4:30*

"And when these things begin to come to pass, then look up, and lift up your heads; for *your redemption* draweth nigh."—*Luke 21:28*

Then Jesus comes as Judge for judgment of the world.

"And the times of this ignorance God winked at; but now commandeth all men every where to repent: Because he hath appointed a day, in the which *he will judge the world* in righteousness by that man whom he hath ordained; whereof he hath given assurance unto all men, in that he hath raised him from the dead."—*Acts 17:30, 31*

Upon His return as the Judge, Jesus will set up His Kingdom and give thrones to His church that they may reign with Him. This is pointed out in the letters to His church. T U

"To him that overcometh will I grant to sit with me in my throne, even as I also overcame, and am set down with my Father in his throne."
—Revelation 3:21

Another scripture testifies to the fact that the saints will reign with Him.

"Do ye not know that the saints shall judge the world? and if the world shall be judged by you, are ye unworthy to judge the smallest matters? Know ye not that we shall judge angels? how much more things that pertain to this life?"
—1 Corinthians 6:2, 3

After examining all the facts, I am satisfied that those sitting upon the thrones in Revelation are the redeemed church. U

"And I saw thrones, and they sat upon them, and judgment was given unto them…"
—Revelation 20:4

Another group of brethren

But let us look at another group of saved people found in the second part of verse 4 of Revelation chapter 20.

"…and I saw the souls of them that were beheaded for the witness of Jesus, and for the word of God, and which had not worshipped the beast, neither his image, neither had received his mark upon their foreheads, or in their hands; and they lived and reigned with Christ a thousand years."*—Revelation 20:4* N U

This second group is just what the scriptures say they are—the people who accepted Jesus during the seven years and died at the hand of the Antichrist. They have waited for the Lord to take His vengeance under an altar in heaven (Revelation 6:9), and are now resurrected to "live and reign with Christ a thousand years." N U

The scripture speaks of yet another group in the next two verses.

"But the rest of the dead lived not again until the thousand years were finished. This is the first resurrection. Blessed and holy is he that hath part in the first resurrection: on such the second death hath no power, but they shall be priests of God and of Christ, and shall reign with him a thousand years."*—Revelation 20:5,6*

So the rest of the dead (the unsaved) do not live again (for judgment) until the thousand years are finished.

From Jesus to the beginning of the Millennium

In Revelation 20:6, a new thought is introduced, that of the *first resurrection.* The first resurrection started when Jesus rose from the dead and has continued on throughout the ages. This includes every believer that has died, received a new body, and gone to be with the Lord. The rapture of the church is part of this ongoing event that concludes with the resurrection of the tribulation saints as Christ returns with His church. Blessed (happy) are those that have part in it for they shall reign with Christ for the thousand years. U

The true *New Age*

The thousand year reign of Christ will be a very interesting period of time. The people who have survived the tribulation period will enter the millennium and continue to live, to have children, and to join together as nations. These nations will live under Jesus' rule with their destinies in His hands. U

Each year the nations will be required to bring Jesus an offering. If they refuse,

He will bring judgment on them (Isaiah 60:1–12, Zechariah 14:16–21). Scripture uses the example of Egypt where it is stated that if they refused to bring their offering, rain would be withheld from their nation for a year.

Jesus said that when He returns as Redeemer, He will ask each believer how they invested the talents entrusted to them. How talents were used during their lifetimes determine the authority they will have during the thousand year reign of Christ. (Matthew 25:20–23). The saints will be working among the people of the world, teaching them about Jesus Christ. Jesus will give them power to rule over the nations with Him.

"And he that overcometh, and keepeth my works unto the end, to him will I give power over the nations: And he shall rule them with a rod of iron; as the vessels of a potter shall they be broken to shivers: even as I received of my Father."—*Revelation 2:26, 27*

Evil unchanged

Revelation goes on to explain what happens at the end of the thousand years.

"And when the thousand years are expired, Satan shall be loosed out of his prison, And shall go out to deceive the nations which are in the four quarters of the earth, Gog and Magog, to gather them together to battle: the number of whom is as the sand of the sea."
—*Revelation 20:7, 8*

Satan is loosed again. He will be given a final opportunity to deceive the nations and lead them to the second battle of Gog and Magog. This battle differs from the battle described in the book of Ezekiel chapter 38. The two battles have different combatants and different conclusions.

The unregenerated

Satan can't deceive the saints who are reigning with Jesus. The Devil will deceive the people of the unregenerate nations. These nations follow Satan and surround the camp of the saints and the city of the Lord. Their efforts are to no avail for fire comes from God and consumes them all. Soon afterwards, Satan is cast into the Lake of Fire and disposed of forever.

"And they went up on the breadth of the earth, and compassed the camp of the saints about, and the beloved city: and fire came down from God out of heaven, and devoured them. And the devil that deceived them was cast into the lake of fire and brimstone, where the beast and the false prophet are, and shall be tormented day and night for ever and ever."
—*Revelation 20:9, 10*

I won't visit his grave

A fitting end for such a vicious foe.

"For ye were sometimes darkness, but now are ye light in the Lord: walk as children of light."
—*Ephesians 5:8*

Chapter 12: Conclusion

My mind returns to 2 Peter as I conclude this writing. Peter, filled with the Holy Ghost, brings new meaning to our lives by asking a question.

"Seeing then that all these things shall be dissolved, what manner of persons ought ye to be in all holy conversation and Godliness."
—*2 Peter 3:11*

With all our heart, soul, mind and strength

Holy conversation means our *whole manner of life* while *godliness* is *the God-ward attitude of your mind* or *devotion to God*. In other words, if these things are true, how should we live our lives? What should our attitude towards God be? Joshua, one of the anointed leaders of Israel, had it right.

"...but as for me and my house, we will serve the LORD."—*Joshua 24:15*

Joshua's statement encapsulates *holy conversation* and *godliness*. It puts devotion to God in clear perspective.

Peter continues by pointing out the reason we should shape our lives into ardent devoted followers of Jesus with another question.

"Looking for and hasting unto the coming of the day of God, wherein the heavens being on fire shall be dissolved, and the elements shall melt with fervent heat?"—*2 Peter 3:12*

Peter looks past the dissolving fire, and continues on to inspire the believer.

"Nevertheless we, according to his promise, look for new heavens and a new earth, wherein dwelleth righteousness. Wherefore, beloved, seeing that ye look for such things, be diligent that ye may be found of him in peace, without spot, and blameless."—*2 Peter 3:13, 14*

The Lord is longsuffering

The Lord's *longsuffering* explains why we are still waiting for the Lord's return.

"And account that the *longsuffering of our Lord is salvation*; even as our beloved brother Paul also according to the wisdom given unto him hath written unto you."—*2 Peter 3:15*

"The Lord is not slack concerning his promise, as some men count slackness; but is *longsuffering to us-ward, not willing that any should perish, but that all should come to repentance."*
—*2 Peter 3:9*

A Mocker

This verse (2 Peter 3:9) has profound meaning to me. In 1965, I was a proclaimed atheist. While staying at a motel in Arcadia, California, I was debating with a close friend concerning the existence of God. In total unbelief, I picked up a Gideon Bible with hopes of pacifying my friend's insistence, that I read to him from the scriptures.

As I opened the Bible, my eyes fell upon 2 Peter 3:9. After reading it, I mocked the idea that the Bible contained promises. I mocked God's Word because, as a child in the Roman church, all I heard were threats from those that supposedly represented the Most High. This memory provoked me to read the New Testament in order to prove that it didn't contain promises, only threats.

After reading the Gospels of Matthew, Mark, and Luke, I found nothing that caught my interest and was about to throw it aside. It seemed repetitious and contradictory. You see, as a natural, unregenerate man, the things of the Spirit seemed foolish to me.

"But the natural man receiveth not the things of the Spirit of God: for they are foolishness unto him: neither can he know them, because they are spiritually discerned. But he that is spiritual judgeth all things, yet he himself is judged of no man."—*1 Corinthians 2:14, 15*

The Beckoning

However, something drove me on to read one more book—the book of John. At the time, I attributed this drive to my own determination and stubbornness. Not long afterwards, I understood this drive to be the Holy Spirit calling and beckoning me to Christ. The first three verses in John chapter 1 fascinated me. In all my 25 years, never had I read such a profound statement.

"In the beginning was the Word, and the Word was with God, and the Word was God. The same was in the beginning with God. All things were made by him; and without him was not any thing made that was made."—*John 1:1–3*

I read these verses over and over again thinking, "How poetic!" As I continued on in the chapter, I came to verse 14.

"And the Word was made flesh, and dwelt among us, (and we beheld his glory, the glory as of the only begotten of the Father) full of grace and truth."—*John 1:14*

Life-changing words

Stunned, I started again at verse one. After reading this section of scripture several more times, the conviction of the Holy Spirit became real to me for the first time in my life. All of a sudden, this wasn't dead religion. The verses were no longer empty words on paper, they were alive. As the Spirit of the Lord witnessed to me, the truth was made clear, and I believed in Jesus.

Kneeling down, I confessed that I was a sinner. I spoke to God by faith, admitting that my nature was contrary to His. I had found no list of sins in the reading I had done up to this point, but I knew I was a sinner. I knew God was real and that made both heaven and hell real! I knew that Jesus had come to save me from hell and offered me eternal life. I knew I needed to change, and realized the power to change myself was beyond my grasp. I confessed my insufficiency to Him.

Nothing but promises

In John 1:3, Jesus said that He had created all things, so I simply asked Him to recreate me. Hadn't He made Peter, Andrew, John, and James, and so many others I had read about into new people? All I asked was that He would do the same for me. I didn't want to become religious, wear robes, and carry beads around as I had seen others do in my youth. I asked for a genuine change that would make it natural for me to follow Jesus.

At that point, I did feel a change in my heart to the center of my being. I told the Lord that I would, from that moment on, be His slave. However, slavery was not what He wanted. Instead, He changed me, setting me free from the slavery of my old nature. I haven't stopped reading the Bible to this day and have found nothing but promises instead of the threats that I had presumed to be there.

The coming promise

One of these promises, the Day of the Coming of Jesus Christ, has been forestalled for almost two thousand years. However, the Bible gives believers a list of events that would precede the promise of His return. This present generation has witnessed the rebirth of Israel as a nation, which the Word of God says will mark the *Last Generation*. We know that no man knows the day or the hour that the Lord will come as a thief in the night, but we are told that we will know the season. O D

"But of the times and the seasons, brethren, ye have no need that I write unto you. For yourselves know perfectly that the day of the Lord so cometh as a thief in the night. For when they shall say, Peace and safety; then sudden destruction cometh upon them, as travail upon a woman with child; and they shall not escape. But ye, brethren, are not in darkness, that that day should overtake you as a thief. Ye are all the children of light, and the children of the day: we are not of the night, nor of darkness."
—*1 Thessalonians 5:1–5*

A clear distinction—Smell the sweetness

Just as we are aware of the end of winter and the beginning of spring by the budding of the trees, the believer will feel the same about the coming of Jesus. However, the unbeliever will not smell the flowers. He will be busy with other things. Here is a serious message concerning two vastly different perspectives about the world in which we live. As the world draws toward the end, it will see peace and safety on the horizon. But believers will see the approaching wrath of God. This will definitely put a clear distinction between the two groups. Both groups are given a strong warning by Jesus Himself.

And take heed to yourselves, lest at any time your hearts be overcharged with surfeiting, and drunkenness, and cares of this life, and so that day come upon you unawares. For as a snare shall it come on all them that dwell on the face of the whole earth."—*Luke 21:34, 35*

This snare will come upon the whole earth. However, believers are told if they take heed to God's Word, it won't be a snare to them. I again must conclude that believers will have knowledge prior to being taken out of the way before the whole of humanity is snared by the judgment (sudden destruction) that will encompass the earth. Jesus continued with His instructions. D N

"Watch ye therefore, and pray always, that ye may be accounted worthy to escape all these things that shall come to pass, and to stand before the Son of man."—*Luke 21:36*

Walking and Watching

This exhortation alerts the believer to watch and pray to be accounted worthy to escape the snare of the whole earth. Accounted worthy? How? I believe being worthy is a very simple thing. As we read a bit ago, the people in the light were told they would be aware of the destruction coming. Therefore, *walking in the light* and *being worthy* are closely related. Being able to *walk in the light* is only accomplished through the guidance of the Holy Spirit.

"But the anointing which ye have received of him abideth in you, and ye need not that any man teach you: but as the same anointing teacheth you of all things, and is truth, and is no lie, and even as it hath taught you, ye shall abide in him. And now, little children, *abide in him*; that, when he shall appear, we may have confidence, and *not be ashamed before him at his coming."—1 John 2:27, 28*

I believe that if we are not ashamed at His Coming, we certainly must be worthy. Therefore if we abide in Him through the guidance of and obedience to His Spirit, we will be in the light and aware of the signs of the times and the seasons, while the whole world will remain unaware of what's really going on. This awareness, coupled with prayer, will give us a close walk with Jesus and the worthiness we need to escape.

More evidence of light and darkness

We are aided in our awareness of the times in which we live by the many Christian newsletters and chronicles regarding the worldwide decline of morals and values. The very existence of these publications is a sign of the times. In stark contrast, the world views these same publications as religious, fanatical tripe. See the difference? I believe God has anointed men and women who warn us every day through these publications, but the world's media believes these are written by sick people. Can you see the conflict of light verses the darkness?

The information generation

An extensive amount of information is inundating us from the secular world. This information is flooding our home and lives through the internet, television, daily newspapers, magazines, and radio. This constant flow of news, unavailable to previous generations, should alert the believer to the corresponding events prophesied in the scriptures. Because of their Biblical perspective, believers will perceive news much differently than their secular neighbors.

Companions in darkness

An unbeliever and a lukewarm Christian are often closely related in their viewpoints. Both may agree that the National ID Card will solve medical and governmental organizational problems. They may also agree with the press and the ruling powers that the word *liberal* means being progressive, and to be free from bigotry. Both may even believe that promoting homosexuality is a civil right and will make everyone happier. They may agree that abortion is morally correct and an acceptable form of birth control. They may even agree that embryo and fetal tissue experimentation is a medical breakthrough. Both groups accept the developments in this country and throughout the world as beneficial to society, even if they are contrary to the teaching of the Bible. Both groups seek progress towards all people of the world getting along together (world peace).

Companion with Jesus

If Jesus wasn't Lord of my life and I didn't obey the Holy Spirit, I would probably feel the same way. I would have sufficient worldly peer pressure around me *to go with the flow* and drop my "fanatical thinking." The sinful actions of society would appear as normal social evolution and not signs of the times. I would also believe that the absence of conflict is peace, and would probably adopt the position of tolerance as the pathway to freedom from guilt.

Walk In the Light

You can see why Paul encouraged the believer to stay in the light.

"For ye were sometimes darkness, but now are ye light in the Lord: *walk as children of light.*" —*Ephesians 5:8*

"Wherefore he saith, Awake thou that sleepest, and arise from the dead, and *Christ shall give thee light.*"—*Ephesians 5:14*

"And that, knowing the time, that now it is high time to awake out of sleep: for now is our salvation nearer than when we believed. The night is far spent, the day is at hand: let us therefore cast off the works of darkness, and *let us put on the armour of light.* Let us walk honestly, as in the day; not in rioting and drunkenness, not in chambering and wantonness, not in strife and envying. But put ye on the Lord Jesus Christ, and make not provision for the flesh, to fulfil the lusts thereof." —*Romans 13:11–14*

Not a time for napping

The encouragement not to sleep is a theme threaded throughout Paul's writings, especially when he deals with the topic of the times and the seasons.

"Therefore let us not sleep, as do others; but let us watch and be sober. For they that sleep sleep in the night; and they that be drunken are drunken in the night."—*1 Thessalonians 5:6, 7*

We understand how to watch; now in this verse Paul adds soberness. To be sober means to be discreet or moderate, *and to be watchful.* We must remember that with Christ we have the ability to see things in the light, to see things as they really are. His Spirit is our guide and teacher! His Word is truly a lamp unto our feet and a light to our path.

Transgressors, transgressors everywhere and not a believer to be seen

As we read earlier, Jesus said that just prior to His coming, life on earth would resemble life on earth in Noah's day. The similarity between the *Days of Noah* and the *Transgressors coming to full* and the present day are remarkable.

"And GOD saw that the wickedness of man was great in the earth, and that every imagination of the thoughts of his heart was only evil continually."—*Genesis 6:5*

"The earth also was corrupt before God, and the earth was filled with violence. And God looked upon the earth, and, behold, it was corrupt; for all flesh had corrupted his way upon the earth. And God said unto Noah, The end of all flesh is come before me; for the earth is filled with violence through them; and, behold, I will destroy them with the earth."—*Genesis 6:11–13*

Compare snapshots

These few verses give us a snapshot of life in the days of Noah. Consider the comparisons. Today, is every man's imagination of the thoughts of his heart only evil? Look around. Is the church lukewarm? Very. If we took a snapshot of life today would it match the one we have of Noah's day? When will the transgressors come to full? Just after the rapture of the church.

Violence?

In the near future, will there be violence upon the face of the earth? Absolutely.

"…for I will call for a sword upon all the inhabitants of the earth, saith the LORD of hosts."—*Jeremiah 25:29*

Violence will be all over the face of the earth and there will be a world war as never seen before among the Gentile nations.

The Ark?

We must remember, even though the transgressors were coming to fullness in the days of Noah, Noah and his wife and children found grace in the eyes of the Lord. They were placed on the ark and saved from the wrath of God.

"And they went in unto Noah into the ark, two and two of all flesh, wherein is the breath of life. And they that went in, went in male and female of all flesh, as God had commanded him: and the LORD shut him in."—*Genesis 7:15, 16*

When they were in the ark, God closed the doors and at that point, all outside the ark were transgressors. The earth was full of them. Will there be an Ark before this last judgment? Yes. The *rapture!* S

The last faithful believer

Can the transgressors come to full if only one Gentile believer remains faithful, not becoming lukewarm? No. Can the king of fierce countenance in Daniel 8:23 stand up? No. There has to be a *departure*, a *snatching away* of all God's people in order for the Antichrist to come.

Dig deeper

I'm looking forward to the day of Jesus Christ. I can't wait until we get to heaven! Remember, there's enough evidence in this book to compel you to search the scriptures for yourself. Don't fall for man's attempts to deceive you with lies.

The great overshadowing

This book is solely my opinion based on my study of the Bible. Studying the Bible and discovering these beliefs has caused me to live my life differently. It has encouraged me to look forward to and focus my life on the coming of Jesus Christ, not on all the events that go on about me. I do note significant events such as birthdays, anniversaries, grandchildren being born, and other important times. But behind them is one great event which overshadows all others, the return of the Lord Jesus Christ. It draws all of my attention, and causes me to endeavor to live a pure life, without spot, while I wait for Jesus Christ.

Past actions—Future judgment—Solid deliverance

The Manasseh Effect testifies of the far-reaching consequences of sin. King Manasseh's actions foreshadowed the coming age of the Antichrist and his dealings with Israel. His actions in the past have set in motion a series of judgments that will change the world.

The remainder of the judgment upon the people of Israel for their part in the *sins of Manasseh* and the judgment on Gentile nations for their rejection of Jesus Christ will happen simultaneously during the last seven years of history. Then the kingdom of God will be established forever. These facts solidify deliverance for the believing Jews and Gentiles in the Church. N R

Seven times seven always equals forty-nine

Remember that the Old Testament book of Leviticus clearly illustrated the Kinsman Redeemer coming on the Feast of Atonement in the forty-ninth year, on the seventh-seventh Sabbath.

The New Testament begins by proclaiming that six-sevens (forty-two generations) had transpired at the birth of Christ as the Passover Lamb. The seven ages of the church will complete 49 generations. All that is left is for Jesus to come as the Redeemer on the Day of Atonement in the forty-ninth generation—the generation in which we now live. C D

Fully persuaded

After more than forty-one years of studying this subject, I am fully persuaded that this is the scenario that the Word of God lays out for the End Times. What should you the reader do? ITD

"Prove all things; hold fast that which is good."
—*1 Thessalonians 5:21*

The Bereans

The Bereans, a group of believers in the book of Acts, were commended by the Apostle Paul.

"...they received the word with all readiness of mind, and searched the scriptures daily, whether those things were so."—*Acts 17:11*

Be as the Bereans were. Search these things out in the scriptures for yourself. Know that the times and the season are upon us!

"Now learn a parable of the fig tree; When his branch is yet tender, and putteth forth leaves, ye know that summer is nigh: So likewise ye, when ye shall see all these things, know that it is near, even at the doors. Verily I say unto you, This generation shall not pass, till all these things be fulfilled."—*Matthew 24:32-34*

"The fig tree putteth forth her green figs, and the vines with the tender grape give a good smell. Arise, my love, my fair one, and come away."—*Song of Solomon 2:13*

Borrowed time

The natural life span for planet earth has run out. *It is living on borrowed time!*

CHURCH
ABA
PRAY
GOD IS LISTENING
24 - 7

"Behold, I stand at the door, and knock: if any man hear my voice, and open the door, I will come in to him, and will sup with him, and he with me."—*Revelation 3:20*

"For whosoever shall call upon the name of the Lord shall be saved."—*Romans 10:13*

"But these are written, that ye might believe that Jesus is the Christ, the Son of God; and that believing ye might have life through his name."—*John 20:31*

Chapter 13: Where are you in all of this?

If this book has awakened in you a desire to know the living God and escape the judgment coming on the world, then read on.

Did you know that you were created to have a relationship with a loving God? He is patiently and lovingly waiting for you to respond to His invitation of salvation. Yes, you can receive forgiveness for your sins and assurance of eternal life through faith in His only Son, the Lord Jesus Christ.

"For God so loved the world, that he gave his only begotten Son, that whosoever believeth in him should not perish, but have everlasting life. For God sent not his Son into the world to condemn the world; but that the world through him might be saved."—*John 3:16-17*

"And this is life eternal, that they might know thee the only true God, and Jesus Christ, whom thou hast sent."—*John 17:3*

You may be asking yourself: "How can I know God?" Man is able to know the true and living God through His Word (that is, the Bible). The Bible reveals God's character and His plan for mankind. It is through reading His Word that we come to a knowledge of the righteousness of God and what He requires of us.

What is it that prevents us from personally knowing God? Our sin has separated us from God—our corruption is to such a degree that we cannot know Him personally and cannot experience His love.

"The heart is deceitful above all things, and desperately wicked: who can know it?" —*Jeremiah 17:9*

"For all have sinned, and come short of the glory of God."—*Romans 3:23*

Man was created to have fellowship with God, but because of his sin (i.e., anything that is against the righteousness revealed in God's Law) he is prevented from that fellowship. This includes anything less than perfect obedience to God's commands.

"For the wages of sin is death; but the gift | of God is eternal life through Jesus Christ our Lord."—*Romans 6:23*

The ultimate result of this death is an eternity in Hell. This spiritual death forces a separation from God. Since people are sinful and God is holy, it is impossible for us to have the relationship and fellowship with the Lord as He originally intended.

What's the solution?

The only solution is Jesus Christ.

"But God commendeth his love toward us, in that, while we were yet sinners, Christ died for us."—*Romans 5:8*

"For he hath made him to be sin for us, who knew no sin; that we might be made the righteousness of God in him."
—*2 Corinthians 5:21*

Jesus became sin for us and took the punishment we deserved. Because of His sacrifice for our sin, we now have available to us a way to have fellowship with Him. He is the only way.

"Jesus saith unto him, 'I am the way, the truth, and the life: *no man cometh unto the Father, but by me.'* "—*John 14:6*

What must I do to be saved?

God made provision for and judged your sin through the sacrifice made by Jesus in your place. But to take advantage of God's provision, you must receive this gift of God by faith, the faith that God is granting to you right now. The goodness of God is leading you to repentance, to turn from darkness (the power of Satan) to God, and place your trust in Jesus Christ as your Lord and Saviour. It is by believing in the Lord Jesus Christ and repenting of your sins that you can have the sin issue settled and enjoy peace with God. What a joy it is to know God personally, to walk with Him, and to look forward to spending eternity with Him.

"But as many as received him, to them gave he power to become the sons of God, even to them that believe on his name."—*John 1:12*

"For by grace are ye saved through faith; and that not of yourselves: it is the gift of God: Not of works, lest any man should boast. For we are his workmanship, created in Christ Jesus unto good works, which God hath before ordained that we should walk in them."
—*Ephesians 2:8-10*

"Then Peter said unto them, 'Repent, and be baptized every one of you in the name of Jesus Christ for the remission of sins, and ye shall receive the gift of the Holy Ghost.' "—*Acts 2:38*

Receive Jesus right now by faith and be reconciled with God forever

Accept Jesus Christ as your Lord and Saviour.

"That if thou shalt confess with thy mouth the Lord Jesus, and shalt believe in thine heart that God hath raised him from the dead, thou shalt be saved. For with the heart man believeth unto righteousness; and with the mouth confession is made unto salvation."—*Romans 10:9-10*

"And the publican, standing afar off, would not lift up so much as his eyes unto heaven, but smote upon his breast, saying, God be merciful to me a sinner."—*Luke 18:13*

Use these words to guide your prayer. The exact words aren't important.

"Heavenly Father, I believe that You sent Jesus to die on the cross, paying for my sins. I also believe that You raised Jesus from the dead, and through His resurrection, I can look forward to eternal life. Forgive me for all I have done wrong that I may be born again.

"I trust Jesus as my Lord and Saviour. Thank You Jesus for coming into my heart and giving me a new life. Amen."

Email or write to us to let us know of your decision so we can share in your joy, and pray for you.

Welcome to God's family!

If you believed God's Word and placed your faith in His Son, congratulations—welcome to His family. All of His children share in His heavenly inheritance! We are heirs to heaven and are promised the eternal pleasure of glorifying God.

As our life here on earth progresses, God will continue to work in our hearts. We are daily being conformed to the image of Christ Himself. We will begin to live lives of righteousness. Obedience to God will not be a burden to us, but rather a joy.

You may wonder, now that you are a Christian, "What now?" Our greatest recommendation for believers, new and old, is fourfold:

1. Find a church where you can hear the preaching of the Word and rejoice in the fellowship of other Christians.

2. Read the Bible, preferably the King James Version (see Addendum, *Which Bible*), to learn about God. Download a yearly reading schedule from www.TheHistoryOfTomorrow.com. You can learn about Jesus by enrolling in Pastor John's *Jesus Life and Ministry* course, and receive a free two-hour study DVD each month to study the life of Jesus in the order the events happened. www. JesusLifeAndMinistry.com

3. Pray to your Father in Heaven to strengthen your faith and increase your love toward Him.

4. Enjoy the blessings given by God in the only Biblically ordained ordinances: baptism and the Lord's Supper (also called communion).

5. Share your faith with others.

All of these will work to encourage and build upon your faith. If you have questions, search the scriptures for yourself, ask your Pastor, or feel free to contact us at our website: www.TheHistoryOfTomorrow.com

May God richly bless you.

The Christian Life NEW TESTAMENT
HOLY BIBLE
CONCORDANCE
RED LETTER EDITION
King James Version
Holy Bible
CAMBRIDGE
HOLY BIBLE
KING JAMES VERSION
BOLD TEXT EDITION
The DEFENDER Study Bible
King James Version
RED LETTER EDITION
FIRST WORD
Holy Bible
The New King James Version

Addendum: Which Bible?

The premise presented in The *Manasseh Effect* is based on the reading of the Bible and taking it literally. The author believes that God said what He meant and meant what He said.

"For ever, O LORD, thy word is settled in heaven."—*Psalm 119:89*

God's Word may be settled in heaven, but it doesn't seem to be settled down here. Or is it?

There are so many Bibles available today it is difficult for believers to be able to determine if one Bible is better than another, or if they are all more-or-less the same. To confuse the issue further, most new versions use commonplace language that can have vague meanings, forcing the Bible reader to depend on men for interpretation and understanding. Relying on men's abilities to be able to distinguish what is accurate and what is error is foolhardy, because men are fallen sinners and cannot possibly know. They must have some ulterior motive for their claim to have this knowledge.

I want to encourage you to read the Bible with full assurance that you do have the Word of God in your hands, preserved the way God intended. It is a wonderful thing when talking to someone about the Lord to be able to hand them the Bible to read instead of a tract or a denominational book. I'm never worried that a seeker of truth will get confused and be lead astray by God's Word. No one ever became a Jehovah's Witness, Muslim, Mormon, Mason, or Roman Catholic by reading the scriptures alone.

It's not the intention here to present an in-depth study of Bible preservation, but merely an overview. You are encouraged to do your own study and to come to your own conclusions.

Did God really preserve His Words?

Preservation of the Words of God is crucially important to our understanding of God's revealed will to us. If we do not have God's Word intact and without error, then we have no reliable source of information about what we must do to be saved. It would also speak rather poorly of a God that claims to have created the universe and yet is unable to preserve His Word. Without His revealed Word, I have no hope—I'll perish. Besides, how can I be judged by His Word if I don't know what it is, or if it is no longer available?

If we have a Bible that has errors, then who could possibly be qualified to say what is correct and what is not? If I didn't believe the Bible was true, I would have no reason to be a Christian, since my faith is based on the very Words of the Bible.

What does the Bible say?

The first step to determine if God preserved His Word is to study what the Bible says about itself. One might argue that basing the reliability of the text on the text itself is circular reasoning, but that is not the case. God proclaims in His Word that His very words are true and unchanging.

According to the Bible, God has guarded and kept His Word.

"The words of the LORD are pure words: as silver tried in a furnace of earth, purified seven times. Thou shalt keep them, O LORD, thou shalt preserve them from this generation for ever."
—Psalm 12:6, 7

Peter walked with Jesus, and was a witness to His transfiguration. Yet Peter states that the Word of God, which is backed by fulfilled prophecy, is more reliable than his first-hand account.

"We have also a more sure word of prophecy; whereunto ye do well that ye take heed, as unto a light that shineth in a dark place, until the day dawn, and the day star arise in your hearts."
—2 Peter 1:19

In John chapter 17, Jesus prays to the Father to set apart believers with the truth of scripture.

"Sanctify them through thy truth: thy word is truth."*—John 17:17*

The Bible is inspired of God.

"All scripture is given by inspiration of God, and is profitable for doctrine, for reproof, for correction, for instruction in righteousness."
—2 Timothy 3:16

Jesus also states in all three gospels that His Word is eternal and unchanging. By contrast, new modern translations are copyrighted, continuously being updated, and re-published.

"Heaven and earth shall pass away: but my words shall not pass away."*—Matthew 24:35, Mark 13:31, Luke 21:33*

Is the Bible completed?

The first verse of Revelation starts out, "The Revelation of Jesus Christ..." With that in mind, Hebrews shows us that the Bible is complete, and that Revelation is the last book.

"God, who at sundry times and in divers manners spake in time past unto the fathers by the prophets, Hath *in these last days* spoken unto us by his Son, whom he hath appointed heir of all things, by whom also he made the worlds."*—Hebrews 1:1, 2*

"In these last days" means the last in succession, or at the end. The last days began with the Church Age. So what it is saying in Hebrews is that Jesus has spoken in the last of the last days. You will remember from *Chapter 1: The Foundational Truth* that all scripture is prophecy, and it all testifies of Jesus Christ. Therefore, the Words of Jesus as recorded by John in Revelation must be the conclusion.

"For I testify unto every man that heareth the words of the prophecy of this book, If any man shall add unto these things, God shall add unto him the plagues that are written in this book: And if any man shall take away from the words of the book of this prophecy, God shall take away his part out of the book of life, and out of the holy city, and from the things which are written in this book."—*Revelation 22:18,19*

Satan's attack on the Bible

It comes as no surprise to me that Satan would do everything in his power to eliminate or undermine the Bible. In the third century A.D., a version of the text was even intentionally altered to conform to the ideologies of the world's philosophers in Alexandria, Egypt. And for centuries the powers in Christianity at Rome intentionally kept God's Word from the common people. They added their own dogmas to keep people in ignorance, preserving the power the church had over them.

But Satan's plan to keep the Word of God from man was defeated by the efforts of faithful men, many of whom were martyred, and by the invention of the printing press. At that very unique point in time, an English translation of God's Word, the Authorized or King James Version, was written. It was a unique time because the translation was pivotal in solidifying the English language, and was translated by an unparalleled group of scholars who were committed to the authority of God's Word. The King James Bible is also unique in that it is the culmination of a line of Bibles based on God's true Word preserved though uncorrupted manuscripts. Additionally, many great men of God gave their lives working to get God's Word into the hands of the common man.

King James did not translate anything; he just licensed the scholars to do the translation. They in return honored the king by naming the translation after him. The influence of the King James Bible on the world has been remarkable, as evidenced by unprecedented revivals in the 17th, 18th, and 19th centuries.

In the late 1800s, Satan started his relentless campaign to flood the world with Bibles based on the intentionally corrupted manuscripts which had originated in Alexandria, Egypt. His intent was and continues to be to undermine the believer's belief in the Bible as being preserved and reliable. When believers lack confidence in the inerrancy of God's Word, the result is a weakened testimony to an unbelieving world.

"Now the serpent was more subtil than any beast of the field which the LORD God had made. And he said unto the woman, *Yea, hath God said,* Ye shall not eat of every tree of the garden?"—*Genesis 3:1*

Satan is a liar. The first thing he said in the Bible undermined God's Word to Eve. He's never bothered to change his tactics because they work so well.

The originals are long gone

Have you ever read a statement of faith from a church or ministry that says something like this: "We believe that the Bible is inerrant in the original autographs." That sounds good, but the statement reveals that whoever wrote it doesn't believe that they have the Bible, and whatever they use is subject to a great deal of interpretation and manipulation. Why? Because the original autographs are long gone. So what their statement implies is that we need a scholar to help us figure out what's left of whatever God might have written.

But does it matter if the original autographs are gone? Consider the account of Moses receiving the Ten Commandments.

"And he gave unto Moses, when he had made an end of communing with him upon mount Sinai, two tables of testimony, tables of stone, written with the finger of God."—*Exodus 31:18*

God Himself wrote on the tables of stone! That was an original autograph if there ever was one. But when Moses descended from the presence of God to deliver the Word to the people, he found them in rebellion and idolatry. Moses became angry and broke the tables. Then God did something most remarkable.

"And the LORD said unto Moses, Hew thee two tables of stone like unto the first: and I will write upon these tables the words that were in the first tables, which thou brakest."—*Exodus 34:1*

So Moses brought down from the mountain a copy of the Ten Commandments, again written by the finger of God. The copies were identical to the originals, and therefore just as reliable. God preserved His Word. He does not depend on man to preserve it for Him.

Here's another example. In Jeremiah 36:18, Jeremiah dictated God's Word to Baruch who wrote the words down with ink in a book. The book was eventually taken to the King, who cut it up with a penknife as it was read and burned it. But that didn't prevent God's Word from being preserved. God just had Jeremiah and Baruch repeat the process, making a perfect duplicate.

"Then the word of the LORD came to Jeremiah, after that the king had burned the roll, and the words which Baruch wrote at the mouth of Jeremiah, saying, Take thee again another roll, and write in it all the former words that were in the first roll, which Jehoiakim the king of Judah hath burned."—*Jeremiah 36:27, 28*

Jeremiah couldn't have recomposed the text the second time any more than he could have composed it the first time; God dictated it to him both times.

Even today, a notarized or authenticated copy is used as a substitute for the original. So an accurate copy is equal in authority to the original. God states in Psalms 12:7 that He will preserve His Word.

King James Bible "revisions"

The 1611 King James Bible went through four editions in the first 27 years after it was printed. These editions included changing the font style from German Gothic to Roman, and fixing typographical errors that found their way into the printing because of human error. Keep in mind that early printing presses were very primitive by today's standards. The type was set by hand, one letter at a time, and the Authorized Version has a lot of letters. In spite of its primitive printing method, corrections of these typographical errors were only needed in about 400 places.

As an example of how errors can get into a manuscript, the book you are reading was created with the aid of a computer and sophisticated software. It has gone through many rewrites and proofing stages. It has been spell-checked repeatedly, and looked at by many people carefully prior to its going to press. Yet in spite of our best efforts, more than likely you have run across typographical errors. So, it's easy to understand how these kinds of errors could be introduced with hand-set type.

Copyrights

Another thing to keep in mind is that all of the modern translations and paraphrases are subject to copyright. That means that the text can't be copied or redistributed without a royalty paid to and permission from the copyright holder. The Derivative Copyright Law states in part: "To be copyrightable, a derivative work must be different enough from the original to be regarded as a 'new work' or *must contain a substantial amount of new material. Making minor changes or additions of little substance to a pre-existing work will not qualify the work as a new version for copyright purposes.*"

Therefore, there must be many text changes, including both additions and deletions, in order to secure a new copyright. Yet new Bibles are being continually developed. Why? Bible printing is big business, and it is quite conceivable that the desire to make money could override concerns for the integrity of the original text.

"And through *covetousness* shall they with feigned words make *merchandise* of you: whose judgment now of a long time lingereth not, and their damnation slumbereth not."—*2 Peter 2:3*

"To the law and to the testimony: *if they speak not according to this word, it is because there is no light in them.*"—*Isaiah 8:20*

If you are reading another translation, that's up to you. We just want you to be aware of the controversy that surrounds God's truth. We hold to the King James Version, for it is the translation that men have given their lives and reputations to preserve. Additionally, it continues to be attacked today by progressives that present their world-changing plans along with their new translations, versions of what they call "God's Word."

It's the message of God's Word that is inerrant. The King James Bible, more than any other translation, best communicates the central theme of the Bible by emphasizing our redemption through the blood of Jesus Christ.

"Who hath delivered us from the power of darkness, and hath translated us into the kingdom of his dear Son: *In whom we have redemption through his blood, even the forgiveness of sins.*"—*Colossians 1:13, 14*

"But now in Christ Jesus ye who sometimes were far off are made nigh by the blood of Christ."—*Ephesians 2:13*

Appendix A—Chart-to-Book References

This list will help you find where the letter references are in the book if you are starting from the chart.

A...........5, 13, 17
B...........9, 13, 26
C...........11, 12, 89
D...........12, 13, 14, 15, 16, 17, 21, 22, 36, 46, 55, 58, 62, 85, 89
E...........9, 13, 14, 17, 26, 31, 78
F...........19, 20, 25, 26, 31, 32, 39
G...........19, 24, 27, 29, 30, 31, 32, 55
H...........29, 32, 55, 56, 57, 58
I...........20, 21, 22, 23, 25, 26, 31, 32, 48
J...........22, 25, 31, 32, 36
K...........26, 31, 36
L...........14, 16, 17, 35, 36, 49, 50, 51, 52
M...........32, 48, 49, 55
N...........1, 25, 31, 32, 33, 35, 36, 39, 57, 59, 62, 76, 78, 80, 85, 88
O...........17, 21, 35, 36, 46, 52, 59, 85
P...........31
Q...........45
R...........32, 35, 65, 66, 67, 79, 88
S...........2, 3, 13, 14, 15, 16, 33, 45, 47, 78, 79, 88
T...........13, 16, 55, 78, 80
U...........77, 79, 80, 81
V...........2, 35, 39, 40, 43
W...........3, 14, 15, 17, 32, 33, 46, 47, 57, 64, 65, 66, 67, 78, 79
X...........25, 26
Y...........9, 27
Z...........11, 14, 15, 16, 25, 31, 36
ITD.......1, 3, 35, 44, 45, 52, 59, 89

Appendix B—Nuclear Proliferation Chart

	US	Russia	UK	France	China	Israel	India	Pakistan	North Korea
WEAPONS									
Stockpile	10,640	16,000	200	350	400?	200	110-150	75	~13
Deliverable	6,390	3,242	200	350	~325	200	110	75	~13
ICBM									
Number	500	497			24				
Warheads	1,320	1,770			24				
Type	MM II: 0	SS-18: 148			DF-5: 24				
	MM III: 500	SS-19: 35							
	MX PK: 12	SS-24: 36							
		SS-25: 300							
		SS-27: 40							
IRBM, MRBM									
Number					100	100	70	100	100
Warheads					100	100	+50	65	8
Type					DF-3: 40	Jericho 1: 50	Prithvi : 70	Shaheen-I: 34	ND-1: 100
					DF-4: 12	Jericho 2: 50	Agni: 20	Shaheen-II: 15	
					DF-21: 48			Ghauri: 50	
SLBM									
Number	360	192	58	64	12	24			
Warheads	2,880	672	~200	384	12	24			
Type	Trident-1: 72	SSN-8: 152	Trident-2: 64	M-4: 48	JL-1: 12	Popeye: 24			
	Trident-2: 288	SSN-18:96		M-45: 16					
		SSN-20:							
		SSN-23:96							
SSBN	Ohio: 15	Delta I: 0 [12]	Vanguard: 4	Inflexible:1	Xia-SSBN: 1	Dolphin: 3			
		Delta III: 6 [13]		Triomphant: 3					
		Delta IV: 6 [7]							
		Typhoon: 1 [6]							
HEAVY BOMBERS									
Number	56 [208]	78							
Weapons	~900 [~2,000]	800							
Type	B-2: 12 [21]	Tu-95H6: 28							
	B-1B:0 [93]	Tu-95H16: 35							
	B-52: 44 [94]	Tu-160: 15							
THEATER BOMBERS									
Number		487		60	150		400	143	
Weapons	1,290	1,500?		60	150	75	+50	10	
Type	F-15	Air Force		M2000N: 60	H-6: 120	F-4	MiG-27: 147	A-5: 49	
	F-16	Tu-22M: 116		60 Etendard: 0	Q-5: 30	f-16	Jaguar: 88	Mirage III: 16	
	F-18	Su-24: 371					M2000: 35	Mirage 5: 52	
		Navy					Su-30: 30	F-16: 25	
		Tu-22M: 58							
		Su-24: 58							
OTHER THEATER AND TACTICAL NUCLEAR WEAPONS									
Weapons		1,850?			120?				
Type		AF 1,200			DF-11				
		SAMs			DF-15				
		Navy: 640			Artillery				
		Aircraft			ADM				
		Missiles							
		Torpedoes							

www.globalsecurity.org/wmd/world/summary.htm • Weapons of Mass Destruction (WMD) • Status of Nuclear Powers and Their Nuclear Capabilities • 01 January 2005

Scripture Index

Genesis
3:1 97
3:7 16
3:15 49
3:21 16
6:5 .... 57, 87
6:11, 12 57
6:11–13 87
7:15, 16 88
7:23 67
10:2–5 40
13:13 57
15:13-16........... 43
15:18 19
18:20, 21 57
18:32 57
19:14 67
19:21, 22 67
22:18 .... 9, 26
38:1–19 12
49:10 .... 48, 49

Exodus
12:1–7 35
12:23 5
20:4–5 .... 23, 32
20:6 23
31:18 97
34:1 98

Leviticus
17:11 6
18:1–25 59
18:22–29 ..... 43, 44
23:40–42 ..... 16, 78
25 .... 13, 23
25:2–5 25
25:8–25 12–13
25:8, 9 .... 11, 16
25:9, 10 15
25:25 16
26 .... 22, 25, 27, 31
26:1–2 22
26:14–18 22–23
26:14–39 22
26:33, 34 25
26:40–42 26

Numbers
14:34 30
19 6

Deuteronomy
4:2 7
12:32 7

Joshua
24:15 83

Judges
18:7 63

1 Samuel
18:10 41

1 Kings
9:1–9 27
9:24 27
22 41

2 Kings
16 28
21:1-17........ 29–30
24:1–3 ... 19, 20, 31
24:7 19

2 Chronicles
8:11 27–28
28 28
28:2 28
28:19 28
28:21 28
28:22–25 29
36:21 25

Ezra
5:1 37

Nehemiah
2:1–6 31

Psalms
12:6, 7 .... 96, 98
16:10 36
24:7 40
75 42
75:8 42–43
76:7–9 27
98: 5–9 73
102:16 77
119:89 95

Proverbs
3:25, 26 46
13:12 66
30:6 7

Song of Solomon
2:13 89

Isaiah
7:14 36
8:20 99
11:11–12 21
26:9 47
53:1–12 36
60:1–12 81

Jeremiah
9:25 38
17:9 91
23:20 1
25:11–12 20
25:15, 16 ..... 42, 62
25:18–26 42
25:27 .... 42, 63
25:28 .... 39, 63
25:29 35, 42, 63, 88
25:30–33 63
25:32 39
25:33 ..... 39, 63–64
29:10 20
30:7 .... 31, 33
30:24 1
36:27, 28 98

Ezekiel
4:4–6 30
38 .... 38, 41–43, 81
38:2 .... 39, 40
38:4 39
38:15 39
38:16 39
38:18–20 ..... 40, 42
38:21 .... 41, 42
39 .... 38, 41, 63
39:2, 3 41
39:6 63
39:6, 7 43

Daniel
7 58
8:23 .... 75, 88
9: 1, 2................ 20
9:3 21
9:4, 5 21
9:10, 11 22
9:21 30

9:22–24 30
9:24 ....31, 32
9:25, 26 ....31, 33
11:31 55

Joel
2:28–32 36

Habakkuk
2:4 50

Haggai
1:5–7 37
2 37

Zechariah
1:2–4 37
1:14–16 37
14:16–21 81

Malachi
3:14–15 48

Matthew
1 .... 11, 14, 16
1:1–3 9
1:16 9
1:17 .... 11, 14, 19
1:18 11
1:30 12
10:6–8 38
10:14 38
10:18 44
10:39 56
13:19 75
13:24–30 14
13:38–43 14
16:24 56
18:21, 22 31
20:28 14
24 ....32, 35
24:2 33
24:11 ....5, 6
24:24 8
24:15 32
24:22 57
24:32-34 ......35, 89
24:35 96
25:20–23 81
25:41 76
27:52, 53 72
28:18–20 38

Mark
4:12 56
13:14 ....56, 57
13:31 96

Luke
8:11 14
10 v
10:21, 22, 24........v
12:45 66
16:22 72
17:26 57
17:28 57
17:26–28 58
17:29, 30 59
17:26–32 67
18:13 92
19:10 13
21:24 .... 17, 20, 21, 46, 52
21:28 .... 19, 21, 55, 64, 79
21:32 ..... 17, 19, 21
21:33 96
21:34–36 85

John
1:1 78
1:1–3 84
1:12 92
1:14 ....78, 84
1:29 5
3:16–17 91
3:18 44
5:39 ....5, 7
7:10–10:21 v
10:28 75
11:43 72
12:24 15
14:6 92
17:3 91
17:17 96
20:31 91

Acts
2:38 92
7:51, 52 69
7:59, 60 69
8:39 75
8:40 75
15:13, 14 49
17:11 .... iv, 89
17:30 .... 1, 38, 79
17:31 . 1, 14, 38, 77
20:28 13
21:21 73
26:18 .... 1, 38, 49

Romans
1:7 68
1:17 50
1:18 35
1:24–27 44
1:28 43
3:23 91
5:8 92
5:9 35
6:23 91
10:9-10.............92
10:13 91
11:25 .... 15, 46, 49, 52
11:26 49
13:11–14 87

1 Corinthians
1:2 68
2:14 56
2:14, 15 84
5:7 5
6:2, 3 80
8:1 v
11:26 45
11:27–28 45
11:29–30 45
13 v
11:32 45
15:25 14
15:51–53 70

2 Corinthians
4:4 ....16, 51
5: 1–4 71
5:6, 7 70
5:8 71
5:21 92
12:2 75
13:5 45

Galatians
2:8 62
3:11 50
3:16 ....9, 26

Ephesians
1:13, 14 .... 13, 79
1:14 65
2 49
2:8–10 92
2:13 99
4:8 72
4:30 .... 14, 79
5:8 .... 83, 87
5:14 87

Colossians
1:13, 14 99
1:16, 17 61

1 Thessalonians
1:9, 10 68
1:10 35
3 70
3:13 .... 68, 79
4:13 .... 69, 70
4:14 .... 70, 79
4:15 71
4:16 .... 15, 65, 71, 75
4:17 .... 65, 71, 74, 75
4:18 .... 72, 75
5:1–3 58
5:1–5 85
5:2, 3 62
5:6, 7 87
5:21 89

2 Thessalonians
2:1–3 .... 52, 73
2:3 .... 73, 74
2:4 .... 32, 56
2:6 74
2:7 74
2:7, 8 73
2:11 .... 41, 51

1 Timothy
3:15 48
6:11 53

2 Timothy
2:15 .... v, 47
3:16 96

Titus
2:13 66

Hebrews
1:1, 2 96
1:3 61
2:12 16
2:14, 15 17
4:9–11 16
8:1–4 6
8:5 6
9:22 6
9:23 .... 6, 7
9:28 74
10:1 6
10:5–7 9
10:10 69
10:12–13 6
10:38 50

1 Peter
4:17, 18 45

2 Peter
1:19 96
2:3 98
2:5–9 67
2:6 44
3:9 .... 83, 84
3:10 .... 53, 60–62
3:11 .... 21, 53, 83
3:12 .... 53, 83
3:13–15 83

1 John
1:7 45
1:9 45
2:27 .... 51–52, 86
2:28 86
3:2–3 66
3:16 v
5:21 .... 24, 25

Jude
1:7 44

Revelation
1 17
1:7 78
2 .... 17, 50
2:20–24 24
2:24 25
2:26, 27 81
3 .... 17, 50
3:1–6 50
3:5 .... 69, 79
3:7–13 50–51
3:17 51
3:20 91
3:21 80
4:1 15
4:1, 2 17
5:6 15
5: 9,10 15
6 .... 41, 78
6:1 77
6:1, 2 .... 40, 41
6: 3, 4................ 41
6:9 80
7 .... 16, 76, 78
7:9, 10 78
7:14 79
11 76
11:1, 2 55
11:3 76
11:18 60
13:4 32
16:13 40
19 78
19:8 .... 69, 79
19:10 7
19:11 .... 77, 78
19:12, 13 77
19:14 79
20:4 80
20:5,6 80
20:7, 8 81
20:9, 10 81
20:11–15 76
20:15 76
22:8 7
22:18, 19 .... 7, 96–97

"For I have not shunned to declare unto you all the counsel of God."—*Acts 20:27*

Index

A.D. 32 31
A.D. 70 .... 32, 39, 48, 49, 55
A.D. 90 ....49, 55
1948 .... 17, 21, 25, 36, 52, 55
1967 ....21, 52
445 B.C. 31
490 ....26, 31, 32
911 58
144,000 76

A

abomination.................. 29, 32, 43, 55, 56, 57
Abraham...............9, 11, 14, 19, 26, 49, 68, 72
Adam 14, 16, 20, 49, 50, 68
Ahab, King...............................24, 29, 30, 41
Ahaz, King 28, 29
altar...................................... 6, 28, 29, 55, 80
America 47, 59
Antichrist.......32, 35, 41, 45, 55, 74, 76, 80, 88
Aquinas, Thomas 50
Ark 67, 88
Ark of the Covenant.................... 6, 27, 28, 29
Aristotle 50
Armageddon..40
Artaxerxes..31
Asaph 42
Ashtaroth......................................24, 27, 29
Asia Minor..47
Assyria 21, 24
atom 60, 61
Atonement, Day of.............. 14, 15, 16, 78, 89

B

Baal (Baalim)............................24, 27–29, 32
Babylon (Babylonian)..............11, 19–21, 25, 26, 31, 32, 36, 48
bestiality...43, 59
beelzebub (dung god)................................32
believers ....v, 1, 32, 36, 45, 48, 49, 56, 59, 65, 66, 68, 70, 86, 89, 93, 95–97
born again 53, 56, 68, 92
bow 40, 41

C

Canada...59
captive (captivity) 5, 24, 28, 72
  Babylonian 19, 20, 21, 25, 26, 32, 36, 48
careless living..63
catechism 23, 24
City of David 27, 28
Christianity........1, 2, 44, 49, 50, 51, 52, 68, 97
church
  age........................ 14, 15, 36, 49, 50, 52, 96
  early 3, 49, 65
  emergent...51
  Gentile 17, 49, 52, 66
commandment.................... 19, 25, 30, 31, 33
  fourth commandment............................23
  second commandment.... 23, 26, 27, 29, 32
  ten commandments.....................23, 97, 98
communion...45, 93
confess 26, 45, 69, 92
conqueror 39, 41
conversation 22, 83
curse............................ 22, 23, 24, 25, 27, 42
Cyrus (King of Persia) 36

D

Damascus 28, 49
Daniel 20–22, 25, 30–33, 54–56, 58, 75, 88
Darby, John..65, 66
David, King........................... 9, 11, 27, 28, 42
Day of the Lord 62, 64, 72
deliverance...2, 3, 33, 35, 46, 57, 65–68, 74, 88
delusion 41, 59, 62
destruction 36, 58, 62, 85
Diana, goddess 68

E

East Gate ... 40
Eastern mysticism ... 48
elect, the ... 57
End Times ... 1, 2, 3, 35, 44, 52, 59, 89
enlightenment ... 50
Ephesus ... 17, 50
Euphrates River ... 19
Europe ... 36, 47, 50, 57
European Union (EU) ... 47
Eve ... 16, 20, 49, 50, 68, 97
explosion ... 61, 62
Ezekiel ... 1, 30, 35, 39, 40–43, 63, 81

F

falling away ... 47, 52, 72–74
fission ... 61
fourteen, fourteenth ... 11, 14, 12
fury ... 1, 39, 42

G

Gabriel ... 30–33
Gehenna ... 76
generation ... 35, 36, 55, 58, 59, 63, 85, 86
  forty-ninth ... 14–17, 21, 36, 62, 89
  forty-second ... 11, 14, 16, 17, 36
  forty-third ... 17
  last ... 21, 22, 55, 58, 67, 85
  seventh ... 17
  twenty-eighth ... 19, 25, 39
Gentile ... v, 1, 2, 32, 17, 35, 38–40, 43–46
Gog ... 39, 40, 63, 81
Gomorrah ... 43, 44, 57, 59
government ... 1, 16, 20, 58, 59
grace ... 20, 45, 57, 68, 76, 78, 84, 88, 92
Greeks ... 39, 68

H

Hades ... 76
Haggai ... 37
Ham ... 49
harpazo ... 75
harvest ... 14–16, 25, 67, 78
Herod ... 36
Hezekiah, King ... 29, 55
Hitler ... 36
Holy of Holies ... 28, 29, 32, 55
Holy Spirit ... 1, 3, 12–14, 36, 43, 49, 51, 52, 65, 70, 79, 84, 86
homosexual (homosexuality) ... 43, 44, 47, 48, 59, 86
horse (horsemen) ... 38–41
horse, white ... 40, 77–79
humanism (humanistic) ... 50, 56

I

icons ... 24, 25, 51
idols ... 1, 22, 24, 25, 27, 29, 30, 45, 51, 55, 68
idolatry (idolatrous) ... 23, 25, 50, 98
image, graven ... 22, 23, 24, 29
iniquity ... 20, 21, 23, 26, 30, 31, 32, 43, 73, 74
Israel
  Antichrist and ... 32, 44, 55, 88
  blindness of ... 46, 49, 52
  carrying away of ... 11, 19, 25
  Holocaust ... 36
  idolatrous worship of ... 23–25
  judged (judgment) ... 13, 22, 26, 31–33, 35, 36, 38–40
  rebirth of ... 36, 85
  Redeemer promised to ... 23
  Masada ... 48, 49
  Messianic Fellowships in ... 47
  mountains of ... 41, 42
  nations against ... 39
  northern Kingdom of ... 24
  Promised Land ... 19, 20, 43, 68
  reconciled ... 33
  Replacement Theology ... 47, 49
  revival of ... 25, 47, 52
  Sabbaths ... 23, 25–27, 78, 89
  scattered (scattering) ... 25, 27, 29, 30
  spiritual warfare ... 36–38, 40
  Temple, preparation to build ... 55
  warned ... 27

J

Jacob's troubles 32
Japheth 40, 49
Jeremiah 1, 20, 25, 30, 35, 38, 39, 42, 62, 63, 98
Jerusalem
- apostles in 49
- belongs to Jews 21, 36, 46
- judgment 30, 31, 38, 39, 42, 52, 55
- idolatry (false worship) 29
- New 51
- todden by Gentiles 17, 20
- Temple in 27, 28, 37, 40
- two witnesses in 76

Jesus (Christ)
- arrives in Jerusalem ....v, 31
- became sin 92
- birth 11, 19, 36, 89
- blood 2, 5–7, 13, 15, 17, 20, 28, 33, 35, 45, 77, 79, 99
- coming for His church.... 2, 3, 8, 14, 17, 22, 46, 52, 57, 64–69, 71–74, 79, 86, 88
- crucified 14, 68
- death 5, 17, 36, 45, 72
- East gate 40
- everlasting kingdom 36
- faith in 50, 91, 93
- High Priest 6
- hope of 62
- Judge 1, 14, 38, 73, 77–79
- Kinsman Redeemer 12–17, 89
- Messiah ....31, 32, , 33, 36, 47, 48, 49, 57
- opens first seal 40, 43
- Passover Lamb 1, 5, 16, 17, 36, 89
- Redeemer 14, 46, 64, 78, 79, 81, 89
- rejection of 38, 45, 88
- resurrection 36, 38, 45, 72, 92
- sacrifice of 6, 9, 14, 20, 53, 68, 92
- Saviour 1, 52, 66, 68, 70, 79,92, 93
- Second Coming 2, 3, 8, 17, 55, 59, 67, 68, 77, 78
- seed 9, 15, 26
- spirit of Prophecy 7
- thief in the night 53, 58, 62, 78, 85
- true peace from 59

Jews
- Messianic 77
- Peter, apostle to 62
- returned ....v, 32, 36, 37
- 144,000 76

Jezebel 24, 25
John (the apostle) 7, 17, 24, 49, 55, 96
Josiah 25
Joshua 43, 83
Joshua, son of Jozadak 48
Jubile 11, 12, 13, 15, 16
Judah (Judeans) 12, 19, 21, 24, 25, 28, 29–32, 36–38, 42, 48, 49, 98
judge 1, 14, 19, 38, 39, 73, 77, 78, 79, 80
judgment
- day of 14, 38, 66, 72, 83
- future 36, 38, 41, 44, 88
- God's 3, 32, 33, 38, 44, 55, 65, 76
- Israel 13, 22, 26, 31–33, 35, 36, 38–40
- of Jerusalem 30, 31, 38, 39, 42, 52, 55
- of nations 32, 35, 38–40, 42–44, 46, 60, 62, 88
- second seal 41, 42
- White Throne 76
- world 1, 2, 14, 38, 42, 43, 50, 67, 72–74, 76, 77, 79, 86, 88

K

King of Assyria 28
King of Syria 28
King Tiglathpileser 28
Kinsman Redeemer, *see Jesus*

L

Lazarus 72
Laodicea 50, 51
Laodicean church 17, 51, 73
Last days 59, 96
Law of The Red Heifer 6
lawgiver 48, 49

love
follow after 53
God, we love.....................................21, 93
God's, for us .... v, 23, 45, 91, 92
lost 50
of Christ 47
of money 66
truth..41, 59
Lot.......................................57, 58, 59, 67

M

Magog.............................. 39, 40, 43, 63, 81
Manasseh 28, 29, 55
effect .... v, 2, 3, 88, 95
sins of.... iv, 19, 24, 26, 29, 30, 31, 32, 45, 55
Masada..48, 49
Mexico 59
Middle East.................................42, 45, 58
Millennium
(see thousand-year reign) 76, 77, 80
Moscow...39
Moses................................ 6, 29, 73, 97, 98
Law of 6, 12, 15, 22, 27

N

National Endowment for the Arts..............59
Noah 1, 40, 49, 57, 67, 68, 87, 88
nuclear 60, 61, 62, 101
parable 15, 35, 89

P

Passover Feast 5, 14, 15
Paul, Apostle.................iv, 1, 2, 38, 47, 49, 52, 56, 58. 62, 68–73, 75, 79, 83, 87, 89
peace and safety.......................58, 59, 62, 85
Pergamos 50
persecute (persecuting) 36, 50, 69
Peter, Apostle.....22, 31, 60, 62, , 67, 83, 84, 96
Pharaoh 27, 36, 42
Philadelphia..50
Promised Land 19, 20, 43, 68
puzzle.......................................3, 11, 19, 42

Q

queen of heaven *(see Ashtaroth)*.................24

R

rapture 64, 65, 66, 67, 70, 72, 74–76, 80, 87, 88
blessed hope of....................................3, 66
caught up.................. 14, 65, 67, 71, 74, 75
harvest 14–16, 67
redemption *(see redeem/redemption)*
redeem (redemption) 55, 64
Day of 13–15, 19, 21, 79
Jesus, our 14, 46, 64, 78, 79, 81, 89
Jubile............................... 11, 12, 13, 15, 16
Kinsman Redeemer.......................12–17, 89
promise of 14
purchased possession....... 13, 15, 64, 65, 79
waiting for 13–15, 68, 72, 74, 83
Redeemer
Jesus our 14, 46, 64, 78, 79, 81, 89
Kinsman 12–17, 89
Promised to Israel 23
Reformation 50, 65
Renaissance..50
repentance 1, 2, 83, 92
restoration 20
resurrection 36, 38, 45, 72, 80, 92
Romans..2, 48, 49
Russia 39, 101

S

Sabbaths.............................23, 25–27, 78, 89
saint...68, 69, 70
Samuel 25, 27
Sardis 50
Satan 1, 7, 13, 14, 51
and angels...36, 76
attack on Bible...97
blinds 51
depths of...24, 25
destroyer 5, 36
his plan 32, 36, 81

father of lies....51
gave over to....16
god of this world....17, 51
power.... 1, 32, 38, 49, 92
seat of....50
Saul, King....25, 41
scattered.... 25, 27, 30, 36, 38, 52
sceptre....48, 49
seal....30
first....40, 41, 43
second....41, 42
Second coming *(see Jesus)*
seed.... 14, 20, 23, 26, 75
seven
seven-sevens....14, 17
churches....17, 49, 50
generations....16
letters....17, 49, 50
months....14, 15
sabbaths....11, 12, 16
weeks....33
years....3, 11. 16, 36, 39, 44, 62, 76, 78, 80, 88
seventy
Sabbaths....25, 26
weeks....30, 31
years.... 3, 20, 21, 26, 30, 31
Shem....49
Shiloh....48, 49
sixty-nine....32
Smyrna....50
Sodom.... 43, 44, 57, 59, 67
Solomon, King....9, 27–29, 30
Soviet Union....60
statues....23
Stephen....69
sword....17, 20, 25, 35, 41–43, 46, 62, 63, 88
synagogue of Satan....51
Syrian....28

T

Tabernacles, feast of....16, 78
Temple (Tabernacle)
Antichrist's....45, 55, 56
ceremonies....24
defilement....28, 29
destroy (desecration)....27, 29, 32, 48, 49
future....51, 55, 56
Jerusalem....27, 28, 37, 40
Heavenly....6
idol in....30, 55
mount....2, 55
second temple....32, 36, 37
third temple....32, 45, 55, 57
terrorism....58
theoryology....35, 44
thermonuclear....61
thief in the night....53, 58, 62, 78, 85
thousand year reign....80, 81
Thyatira....24, 50
tolerance....51, 58, 87
tree of life....66, 71
Tribulation....31–33, 50, 57, 66, 76, 78, 80
trumpet
Day of Atonement....15, 16
Jubile....11, 12, 15, 16
last....70
Revelation....17
TNT....61, 62
Tubal....39, 40
twenty-eight....24
Tyndale, William....65

U

United States....47, 50, 57–59, 63
USA....3

W
war
cold war 60
global 41–43, 88
Jesus makes.....................................77, 79
Middle East 45
nations devastated by............................44
on terror 58
World War II 36
Yom Kipper 2
warheads..60, 101
weapons 60, 61, 62, 101
weeks..30, 31, 33
world peace......................................58, 59, 86
wrath, God's 1, 2, 35, 46, 55
years
483 ....33, 36
490 ....26, 31, 32

Z
Zechariah...37, 38
Zidonian 24

You can't tell a book by its cover. So, *read* the Bible!

"Sanctify them through thy truth: thy word is truth."—*John 17:17*

"O earth, earth, earth, hear the word of the LORD."—*Jeremiah 22:29*

"For the bread of God is He which cometh down from heaven, and giveth life unto the world."
—*John 6:33*

"The words of the LORD are pure words: as silver tried in a furnace of earth, purified seven times. Thou shalt keep them, O LORD, thou shalt preserve them from this generation for ever."
—*Psalm 12:6–7*

Read Through the Bible in One Year

JANUARY

1	❑ Genesis 1–3	❑ John 1
2	❑ Genesis 4–7	
3	❑ Genesis 8–9	❑ John 2
4	❑ Genesis 10–11	
5	❑ Genesis 12–13	❑ John 3
6	❑ Genesis 14–15	
7	❑ Genesis 16–18	❑ John 4
8	❑ Genesis 19–20	
9	❑ Genesis 21–23	❑ John 5
10	❑ Genesis 24–25	
11	❑ Genesis 26–27	❑ John 6
12	❑ Genesis 28–29	
13	❑ Genesis 30–31	❑ John 7
14	❑ Genesis 32–33	
15	❑ Genesis 34–35	❑ John 8
16	❑ Genesis 36–37	
17	❑ Genesis 38–39	❑ John 9
18	❑ Genesis 40–42	
19	❑ Genesis 43–46	❑ John 10
20	❑ Genesis 47–50	
21	❑ Exodus 1–2	❑ John 11
22	❑ Exodus 3–5	
23	❑ Exodus 6–7	❑ John 12
24	❑ Exodus 8–9	
25	❑ Exodus 10–11	❑ John 13
26	❑ Exodus 12–13	
27	❑ Exodus 14–16	❑ John 14
28	❑ Exodus 17–19	
29	❑ Exodus 20–22	❑ John 15
30	❑ Exodus 23–25	
31	❑ Exodus 26–28	❑ John 16

FEBRUARY

1	❑ Exodus 29–31	
2	❑ Exodus 32–34	❑ John 17
3	❑ Exodus 35–37	
4	❑ Exodus 38–40	❑ John 18
5	❑ Leviticus 1–3	
6	❑ Leviticus 4–6	❑ John 19
7	❑ Leviticus 7–9	
8	❑ Leviticus 10–12	❑ John 20
9	❑ Leviticus 13–15	
10	❑ Leviticus 16–18	❑ John 21
11	❑ Leviticus 19–21	
12	❑ Leviticus 22–24	❑ Romans 1
13	❑ Leviticus 25	
14	❑ Leviticus 26–27	❑ Romans 2
15	❑ Numbers 1–3	
16	❑ Numbers 4–6	❑ Romans 3
17	❑ Numbers 7–8	
18	❑ Numbers 9–11	❑ Romans 4
19	❑ Numbers 12–14	
20	❑ Numbers 15–17	❑ Romans 5
21	❑ Numbers 18–20	
22	❑ Numbers 21–23	❑ Romans 6
23	❑ Numbers 24–26	
24	❑ Numbers 27–29	❑ Romans 7
25	❑ Numbers 30–32	
26	❑ Numbers 33–35	❑ Romans 8
27	❑ Numbers 36	
28	❑ Deuteronomy 1–3	❑ Romans 9

MARCH

1	❑ Deuteronomy 4–6	
2	❑ Deuteronomy 7–9	❑ Romans 10
3	❑ Deuteronomy 10–11	
4	❑ Deuteronomy 12–14	❑ Romans 11
5	❑ Deuteronomy 15–16	
6	❑ Deuteronomy 17–18	❑ Romans 12
7	❑ Deuteronomy 19–20	
8	❑ Deuteronomy 21–22	❑ Romans 13–14
9	❑ Deuteronomy 23–24	
10	❑ Deuteronomy 25–26	❑ Romans 15
11	❑ Deuteronomy 27–28	
12	❑ Deuteronomy 29–31	❑ Romans 16
13	❑ Deuteronomy 32–34	
14	❑ Joshua 1–3	❑ I Corinthians 1–2
15	❑ Joshua 4–6	
16	❑ Joshua 7–9	❑ I Corinthians 3–4
17	❑ Joshua 10–12	
18	❑ Joshua 13–14	❑ I Corinthians 5–6
19	❑ Joshua 15–16	
20	❑ Joshua 17–18	❑ I Corinthians 7–8
21	❑ Joshua 19–20	
22	❑ Joshua 21–22	❑ I Corinthians 9–10
23	❑ Joshua 23–24	
24	❑ Judges 1–3	❑ I Corinthians 11–12
25	❑ Judges 4–6	
26	❑ Judges 7–8	❑ I Corinthians 13–14
27	❑ Judges 9–10	
28	❑ Judges 11–12	❑ I Corinthians 15–16
29	❑ Judges 13–14	
30	❑ Judges 15–16	❑ II Corinthians 1–2
31	❑ Judges 17–18	

APRIL

1	❑ Judges 19–21	❑ II Corinthians 3–4
2	❑ Ruth	
3	❑ I Samuel 1–2	❑ II Corinthians 5–6
4	❑ I Samuel 3–4	
5	❑ I Samuel 5–6	❑ II Corinthians 7–8
6	❑ I Samuel 7–10	
7	❑ I Samuel 11–13	❑ II Corinthians 9–10
8	❑ I Samuel 14–16	
9	❑ I Samuel 17–19	❑ II Corinthians 11–13
10	❑ I Samuel 20–22	
11	❑ I Samuel 23–25	❑ Matthew 1
12	❑ I Samuel 26–27	
13	❑ I Samuel 28–29	❑ Matthew 2
14	❑ I Samuel 30–31	
15	❑ II Samuel 1–3	❑ Matthew 3
16	❑ II Samuel 4–6	
17	❑ II Samuel 7–8	❑ Matthew 4
18	❑ II Samuel 9–11	
19	❑ I Samuel 12–14	❑ Matthew 5
20	❑ II Samuel 15–16	
21	❑ II Samuel 17–18	❑ Matthew 6
22	❑ II Samuel 19–20	
23	❑ II Samuel 21–22	❑ Matthew 7
24	❑ II Samuel 23–24	
25	❑ I Kings 1–3	❑ Matthew 8
26	❑ I Kings 4–6	
27	❑ I Kings 7–9	❑ Matthew 9
28	❑ I Kings 10–12	
29	❑ I Kings 13–15	❑ Matthew 10
30	❑ I Kings 16–18	

M A Y

1	❑ I Kings 19–20	❑ Matthew 11
2	❑ I Kings 21–22	
3	❑ II Kings 1–3	❑ Matthew 12
4	❑ II Kings 4–6	
5	❑ II Kings 7–9	❑ Matthew 13
6	❑ II Kings 10–12	
7	❑ II Kings 13–15	❑ Matthew 14
8	❑ II Kings 16–18	
9	❑ II Kings 19–20	❑ Matthew 15
10	❑ II Kings 21–22	
11	❑ II Kings 23–24	❑ Matthew 16
12	❑ II Kings 25	
13	❑ I Chronicles 1–2	❑ Matthew 17
14	❑ I Chronicles 3–4	
15	❑ I Chronicles 5–6	❑ Matthew 18
16	❑ I Chronicles 7–9	
17	❑ I Chronicles 10–12	❑ Matthew 19
18	❑ I Chronicles 13–15	
19	❑ I Chronicles 16–18	❑ Matthew 20
20	❑ I Chronicles 19–21	
21	❑ I Chronicles 22–23	❑ Matthew 21
22	❑ I Chronicles 24–25	
23	❑ I Chronicles 26–27	❑ Matthew 22
24	❑ I Chronicles 28–29	
25	❑ II Chronicles 1–3	❑ Matthew 23
26	❑ II Chronicles 4–6	
27	❑ II Chronicles 7–9	❑ Matthew 24
28	❑ II Chronicles 10–12	
29	❑ II Chronicles 13–14	❑ Matthew 25
30	❑ II Chronicles 15–16	
31	❑ II Chronicles 17–18	❑ Matthew 26

J U N E

1	❑ II Chronicles 19–20	
2	❑ II Chronicles 21–22	❑ Matthew 27
3	❑ II Chronicles 23–25	
4	❑ II Chronicles 26–28	❑ Matthew 28
5	❑ II Chronicles 29–31	
6	❑ II Chronicles 32–34	❑ Galatians 1–2
7	❑ II Chronicles 35–36	
8	❑ Ezra 1–3	❑ Galatians 3–4
9	❑ Ezra 4–6	
10	❑ Ezra 7–8	❑ Galatians 5–6
11	❑ Ezra 9–10	
12	❑ Nehemiah 1–3	❑ Ephesians 1–2
13	❑ Nehemiah 4–5	
14	❑ Nehemiah 6–7	❑ Ephesians 3–4
15	❑ Nehemiah 8–9	
16	❑ Nehemiah 10–11	❑ Ephesians 5–6
17	❑ Nehemiah 12–13	
18	❑ Esther 1–3	❑ Philippians 1–2
19	❑ Esther 4–6	
20	❑ Esther 7–10	❑ Philippians 3–4
21	❑ Job 1–3	
22	❑ Job 4–6	❑ Colossians 1–2
23	❑ Job 7–9	
24	❑ Job 10–12	❑ Colossians 3–4
25	❑ Job 13–15	
26	❑ Job 16–18	❑ Mark 1
27	❑ Job 19–21	
28	❑ Job 22–24	❑ Mark 2
29	❑ Job 25–27	
30	❑ Job 28–30	❑ Mark 3

J U L Y

1	❑ Job 31–33	
2	❑ Job 34–36	❑ Mark 4
3	❑ Job 37–39	
4	❑ Job 40–42	❑ Mark 5
5	❑ Psalms 1–3	
6	❑ Psalms 4–6	❑ Mark 6
7	❑ Psalms 7–9	
8	❑ Psalms 10–12	❑ Mark 7
9	❑ Psalms 13–15	
10	❑ Psalms 16–18	❑ Mark 8
11	❑ Psalms 19–21	
12	❑ Psalms 22–24	❑ Mark 9
13	❑ Psalms 25–27	
14	❑ Psalms 28–30	❑ Mark 10
15	❑ Psalms 31–33	
16	❑ Psalms 34–36	❑ Mark 11
17	❑ Psalms 37–39	
18	❑ Psalms 40–42	❑ Mark 12
19	❑ Psalms 43–45	
20	❑ Psalms 46–48	❑ Mark 13
21	❑ Psalms 49–50	
22	❑ Psalms 51–53	❑ Mark 14
23	❑ Psalms 54–55	
24	❑ Psalms 56–58	❑ Mark 15
25	❑ Psalms 59–60	
26	❑ Psalms 61–63	❑ Mark 16
27	❑ Psalms 64–65	
28	❑ Psalms 66–68	❑ I Thess. 1–2
29	❑ Psalms 69–70	
30	❑ Psalms 71–73	❑ I Thess. 3–4
31	❑ Psalms 74–75	

A U G U S T

1	❑ Psalms 76–78	❑ I Thess. 5
2	❑ Psalms 79–80	
3	❑ Psalms 81–83	❑ II Thess. 1–2
4	❑ Psalms 84–85	
5	❑ Psalms 86–88	❑ II Thess. 3
6	❑ Psalms 89–90	
7	❑ Psalms 91–93	❑ I Timothy 1–2
8	❑ Psalms 94–95	
9	❑ Psalms 96–97	❑ I Timothy 3–4
10	❑ Psalms 98–99	
11	❑ Psalms 100–101	❑ I Timothy 5–6
12	❑ Psalms 102–103	
13	❑ Psalms 104–105	❑ II Timothy 1–2
14	❑ Psalms 106–108	
15	❑ Psalms 109–110	❑ II Timothy 3–4
16	❑ Psalms 111–113	
17	❑ Psalms 114–115	❑ Titus 1–3
18	❑ Psalms 116–118	
19	❑ Psalms 119: 1–80	❑ Philemon
20	❑ Psalms 119: 81–176	
21	❑ Psalms 120–121	❑ Luke 1
22	❑ Psalms 122–124	
23	❑ Psalms 125–126	❑ Luke 2
24	❑ Psalms 127–129	
25	❑ Psalms 130–131	❑ Luke 3
26	❑ Psalms 132–134	
27	❑ Psalms 135–136	❑ Luke 4
28	❑ Psalms 137–138	
29	❑ Psalms 139–140	❑ Luke 5
30	❑ Psalms 141–142	
31	❑ Psalms 143–144	❑ Luke 6

SEPTEMBER

1	❑ Psalms 145–146	
2	❑ Psalms 147–148	❑ Luke 7
3	❑ Psalms 149–150	
4	❑ Proverbs 1–2	❑ Luke 8
5	❑ Proverbs 3–4	
6	❑ Proverbs 5–6	❑ Luke 9
7	❑ Proverbs 7–8	
8	❑ Proverbs 9–10	❑ Luke 10
9	❑ Proverbs 11–12	
10	❑ Proverbs 13–14	❑ Luke 11
11	❑ Proverbs 15–16	
12	❑ Proverbs 17–18	❑ Luke 12
13	❑ Proverbs 19–20	
14	❑ Proverbs 21–22	❑ Luke 13
15	❑ Proverbs 23–24	
16	❑ Proverbs 25–26	❑ Luke 14
17	❑ Proverbs 27–28	
18	❑ Proverbs 29–31	❑ Luke 15
19	❑ Ecclesiastes 1–2	
20	❑ Ecclesiastes 3–4	❑ Luke 16
21	❑ Ecclesiastes 5–6	
22	❑ Ecclesiastes 7–8	❑ Luke 17
23	❑ Ecclesiastes 9–10	
24	❑ Ecclesiastes 11–12	❑ Luke 18
25	❑ Song of Solomon 1–4	
26	❑ Song of Solomon 5–8	❑ Luke 19
27	❑ Isaiah 1–3	
28	❑ Isaiah 4–6	❑ Luke 20
29	❑ Isaiah 7–9	
30	❑ Isaiah 10–12	❑ Luke 21

OCTOBER

1	❑ Isaiah 13–15	
2	❑ Isaiah 16–18	❑ Luke 22
3	❑ Isaiah 19–20	
4	❑ Isaiah 21–22	❑ Luke 23
5	❑ Isaiah 23–24	
6	❑ Isaiah 25–26	❑ Luke 24
7	❑ Isaiah 27–28	
8	❑ Isaiah 29–30	❑ Acts 1–3
9	❑ Isaiah 31–32	
10	❑ Isaiah 33–34	❑ Acts 4–6
11	❑ Isaiah 35–36	
12	❑ Isaiah 37–38	❑ Acts 7–8
13	❑ Isaiah 39–40	
14	❑ Isaiah 41–42	❑ Acts 9–10
15	❑ Isaiah 43–44	
16	❑ Isaiah 45–46	❑ Acts 11–12
17	❑ Isaiah 47–48	
18	❑ Isaiah 49–50	❑ Acts 13–14
19	❑ Isaiah 51–52	
20	❑ Isaiah 53–54	❑ Acts 15–16
21	❑ Isaiah 55–56	
22	❑ Isaiah 57–58	❑ Acts 17–18
23	❑ Isaiah 59–60	
24	❑ Isaiah 61–62	❑ Acts 19–20
25	❑ Isaiah 63–64	
26	❑ Isaiah 65–66	❑ Acts 21–22
27	❑ Jeremiah 1–3	
28	❑ Jeremiah 4–6	❑ Acts 23–24
29	❑ Jeremiah 7–9	
30	❑ Jeremiah 10–12	❑ Acts 25–26
31	❑ Jeremiah 13–14	

NOVEMBER

1	❑ Jeremiah 15–17	❑ Acts 27–28
2	❑ Jeremiah 18–19	
3	❑ Jeremiah 20–22	❑ Hebrews 1–2
4	❑ Jeremiah 23–24	
5	❑ Jeremiah 25–27	❑ Hebrews 3–4
6	❑ Jeremiah 28–29	
7	❑ Jeremiah 30–32	❑ Hebrews 5–6
8	❑ Jeremiah 33–34	
9	❑ Jeremiah 35–37	❑ Hebrews 7–8
10	❑ Jeremiah 38–39	
11	❑ Jeremiah 40–42	❑ Hebrews 9–10
12	❑ Jeremiah 43–44	
13	❑ Jeremiah 45–47	❑ Hebrews 11–13
14	❑ Jeremiah 48–49	
15	❑ Jeremiah 50–52	❑ James 1–2
16	❑ Lamentations 1–2	
17	❑ Lamentations 3–5	❑ James 3–5
18	❑ Ezekiel 1–3	
19	❑ Ezekiel 4–5	❑ I Peter 1–2
20	❑ Ezekiel 6–8	
21	❑ Ezekiel 9–10	❑ I Peter 3–4
22	❑ Ezekiel 11–13	
23	❑ Ezekiel 14–15	❑ I Peter 5
24	❑ Ezekiel 16–18	
25	❑ Ezekiel 19–20	❑ II Peter 1–2
26	❑ Ezekiel 21–23	
27	❑ Ezekiel 24–25	❑ II Peter 3
28	❑ Ezekiel 26–28	
29	❑ Ezekiel 29–30	❑ I John 1–2
30	❑ Ezekiel 31–33	

DECEMBER

1	❑ Ezekiel 34–35	❑ I John 3–5
2	❑ Ezekiel 36–38	
3	❑ Ezekiel 39–40	❑ II John
4	❑ Ezekiel 41–42	
5	❑ Ezekiel 43–44	❑ III John
6	❑ Ezekiel 45–46	
7	❑ Ezekiel 47–48	❑ Jude
8	❑ Daniel 1–3	
9	❑ Daniel 4–6	❑ Revelation 1
10	❑ Daniel 7–8	
11	❑ Daniel 9–10	❑ Revelation 2–3
12	❑ Daniel 11–12	
13	❑ Hosea 1–3	❑ Revelation 4–5
14	❑ Hosea 4–6	
15	❑ Hosea 7–8	❑ Revelation 6–7
16	❑ Hosea 9–11	
17	❑ Hosea 12–14	❑ Revelation 8–9
18	❑ Joel	
19	❑ Amos 1–3	❑ Revelation 10–11
20	❑ Amos 4–6	
21	❑ Amos 7–9	❑ Revelation 12
22	❑ Obadiah–Jonah	
23	❑ Micah 1–3	❑ Revelation 13–14
24	❑ Micah 4–7	
25	❑ Nahum–Habakkuk	❑ Revelation 15–16
26	❑ Zephaniah–Haggai	
27	❑ Zechariah 1–3	❑ Revelation 17–18
28	❑ Zechariah 4–7	
29	❑ Zechariah 8–11	❑ Revelation 19–20
30	❑ Zechariah 12–14	
31	❑ Malachi	❑ Revelation 21–22

Download an Acrobat version of the Yearly Bible Reading Schedule at: www.RadioFreeChurch.com.

Jesus Life and Ministry FREE Bible School Courses

- **Increase your understanding of the Bible and develop a closer walk with Jesus in the study of His Word!**

- **Paced, subscription courses on DVD, with the teaching of John Higgins and accompanying slides.**

- **The complete course is presented in two parts—The first two years of Jesus' ministry and the last 18 months of Jesus' life on earth.**

- **A DVD will be sent every month at no cost (15 total); at the end of 15 months you will have completed the first course.**

- **Each course is also offered as a college class of three credit hours for a fee.**

Study the Life of Christ in the order that the events happened.

The death and resurrection of Jesus is the foundation of our salvation. Our sins are paid for at the cross and our pardon is granted to us by His resurrection. The study of The Life of Jesus brings us spiritual growth.

As we study His life in the order that the events took place, we gain a new world of understanding. We see Jesus as the Messiah doing exactly as His Father commanded. We see the reason for His messages, His miracles, the events of His life, and His teachings as they come together in a wonderful, revelatory form.

As we learn of the milestone events and put them in order, the events leading up to and the events soon after come to memory. We will see Him as He lived and followed His Fathers will. This has helped me to understand the way God makes all things work together for my good. Faith grows as we grow in Him.

Course One:
The Life of Christ I (The first two years)
The Life of Christ I covers His first two years which are broken up into three main sections. First, the first six months from the baptism of John through the woman at the well. Second, Jesus' first six months in Galilee. From the nobleman's son being healed through the calling of Matthew. Third, we see His second year, from Bethesda through John and James wanting to burn the village and His rejection in Samaria.

Course Two:
The Life of Christ II
(The last eighteen months)

The Life of Christ II covers His last eighteen months which begins in Jerusalem at the feast of Tabernacles. We continue following His life through the appointing of the seventy in the country side of Judea. We watch His movements as He moves about Judah and Perea, passing through Jericho into Jerusalem for the final week leading up to His death and resurrection. We carefully examine all events throughout Jesus' life including His Resurrected Life for the 40 days after He arose.

We are sure that all who study Jesus' Life will grow in their spiritual life in Him.

Jesus Life and Ministry is a resource dedicated to your growth as a Christian by the study of the Word of God.

We offer paced Bible School Courses on DVD taught by Pastor John Higgins of Calvary Chapel Tri-City, Tempe, Arizona. You will gain new insights in God's Word and rejuvenate your love for the Lord through John's Bible teaching. Take advantage of this opportunity to increase your understanding of the Bible and develop a closer walk with Jesus in the study of His Word.

Study at Your Own Pace

A DVD will be sent every month; at the end of 12 months you will have completed one course. Studies are also available online. You are encouraged to take a exam and earn 3 college credits from the Maranatha Bible College. Course credits earned are recognized by several institutions including Maranatha Bible College, an extension campus of Calvary Chapel Bible College in Murrieta, California.

"...freely ye have received, freely give."
—*Matthew 10:8*

The courses are free with no shipping, handling, or hidden charges. If God lays on your heart to contribute to costs of production and shipping, please feel free to do so. If you want college credit, the cost is $80 per credit hour.

All you have to do to enroll is fill out and submit the online application (www.JesusLifeAndMinistry.com), and the first lesson will soon be on its way to you. Or you can print the application and send it to:

Jesus Life and Ministry Courses
2334 E. Southern Ave., Tempe, Arizona 85282 USA.

The course Syllabus can be downloaded from www.JesusLifeAndMinistry.com.

"Take my yoke upon you, and learn of me; for I am meek and lowly in heart: and ye shall find rest unto your souls."—*Matthew 11:29*

www.JesusLifeAndMinistry.com

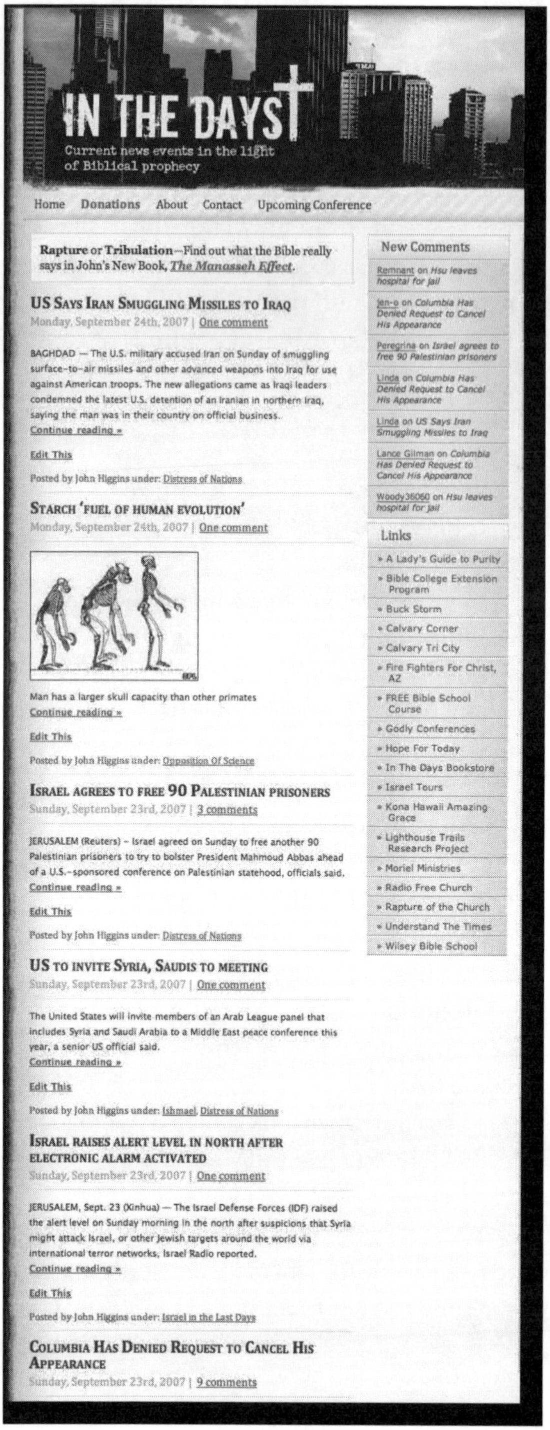

IN THE DAYS

Current news events in the light of Biblical prophecy

Home Donations About Contact Upcoming Conference

Rapture or Tribulation—Find out what the Bible really says in John's New Book, ***The Manasseh Effect***.

US Says Iran Smuggling Missiles to Iraq

Monday, September 24th, 2007 | One comment

BAGHDAD — The U.S. military accused Iran on Sunday of smuggling surface-to-air missiles and other advanced weapons into Iraq for use against American troops. The new allegations came as Iraqi leaders condemned the latest U.S. detention of an Iranian in northern Iraq, saying the man was in their country on official business.

Continue reading »

Edit This

Posted by John Higgins under: Distress of Nations

Starch 'fuel of human evolution'

Monday, September 24th, 2007 | One comment

Man has a larger skull capacity than other primates

Continue reading »

Edit This

Posted by John Higgins under: Opposition Of Science

Israel agrees to free 90 Palestinian prisoners

Sunday, September 23rd, 2007 | 3 comments

JERUSALEM (Reuters) – Israel agreed on Sunday to free another 90 Palestinian prisoners to try to bolster President Mahmoud Abbas ahead of a U.S.-sponsored conference on Palestinian statehood, officials said.

Continue reading »

Edit This

Posted by John Higgins under: Distress of Nations

US to invite Syria, Saudis to meeting

Sunday, September 23rd, 2007 | One comment

The United States will invite members of an Arab League panel that includes Syria and Saudi Arabia to a Middle East peace conference this year, a senior US official said.

Continue reading »

Edit This

Posted by John Higgins under: Ishmael, Distress of Nations

Israel raises alert level in north after electronic alarm activated

Sunday, September 23rd, 2007 | One comment

JERUSALEM, Sept. 23 (Xinhua) — The Israel Defense Forces (IDF) raised the alert level on Sunday morning in the north after suspicions that Syria might attack Israel, or other Jewish targets around the world via international terror networks, Israel Radio reported.

Continue reading »

Edit This

Posted by John Higgins under: Israel in the Last Days

Columbia Has Denied Request to Cancel His Appearance

Sunday, September 23rd, 2007 | 9 comments

New Comments

Remnant on *Hsu leaves hospital for jail*

jen-o on *Columbia Has Denied Request to Cancel His Appearance*

Peregrina on *Israel agrees to free 90 Palestinian prisoners*

Linda on *Columbia Has Denied Request to Cancel His Appearance*

Linda on *US Says Iran Smuggling Missiles to Iraq*

Lance Gilman on *Columbia Has Denied Request to Cancel His Appearance*

Woody36060 on *Hsu leaves hospital for jail*

Links

- A Lady's Guide to Purity
- Bible College Extension Program
- Buck Storm
- Calvary Corner
- Calvary Tri City
- Fire Fighters For Christ, AZ
- FREE Bible School Course
- Godly Conferences
- Hope For Today
- In The Days Bookstore
- Israel Tours
- Kona Hawaii Amazing Grace
- Lighthouse Trails Research Project
- Moriel Ministries
- Radio Free Church
- Rapture of the Church
- Understand The Times
- Wilsey Bible School

IN THE DAYS

Current news events in the light of Biblical prophecy.

InTheDays.com

Today's bazaar headlines tell the story of the world's rapid deterioration into apostasy and depravity. InTheDays.com is designed to keep the believers' eyes looking up, and encouraging the heart by the peace from the scriptures.

"Thou wilt keep him in perfect peace, whose mind is stayed on thee: because he trusteth in thee."—*Isaiah 26:3*

We are creatures that look for directions and follow them to find our desired destinations. The Lord has left us many Biblical signs that will lead the believer to the Day of the Lord. If we follow them.

Therefore, we search the world's news for information that match up with the signs foretold in the scriptures and list them by category on this site.

Our desire is to equip the saints with information that will enable them to be an informed and effective witness for Jesus. In addition, the coming of the Lord Jesus is eminent and that the believer is warned to be ready.

We hope you enjoy your visit and use the information to win many to Jesus before He returns for His Church.

Radio Free Church

"The Word of God is not bound."—*2 Timothy 2:9*

RadioFreeChurch.com

Radio Free Church is for all that have ears to hear, and that love the Truth. We believe the day of the Lord will come in this generation, so we cry out to warn of God's judgment and the hope of redemption. The time is fast approaching where true believers may be forced underground to avoid persecution; nations will attempt to restrict the preaching and teaching of God's Word, but the Word of God cannot be bound. Therefore, we are constrained to cry out for the Truth—God's Word is truth.

Radio Free Church is an online resource to watch or listen to God's Word 24-hours a day from anywhere in the world. Select messages by speaker, conference, subject, topic. Or just sit back and watch featured messages and be edified in the Lord.

Speakers will include David Hocking, Jacob Prasch, Roger Oakland, John Higgins, and many others. We are taking advantage of the available technology to reach the world for the Lord Jesus Christ. Jeremiah cried out to his generation:

"And thou shalt swear, The LORD liveth, in truth, in judgment, and in righteousness; and the nations shall bless themselves in him, and in him shall they glory."—*Jeremiah 4:2*

"And they bend their tongues like their bow for lies: but they are not valiant for the truth upon the earth; for they proceed from evil to evil, and they know not me, saith the LORD."
—*Jeremiah 9:3*

InTheDaysBookstore

Biblical resources to assist you in your personal study of God's Word. Visit www.ITDStore.com to order.

Biblical Studies

I Corinthians

Bible School Class taught by John Higgins. Corinth was a thriving commercial center and a very corrupt city. Paul went there on his second missionary journey, and later wrote to the church there to deal with their problems.

Fall 2005. 13 Lessons on 4 Video DVDs.

The Wanderings

Teaching by John Higgins. The Wanderings, taken from Exodus, is a step-by-step disciple course from the Lord to help us avoid the same mistakes made by the Israelites after coming out of Egypt. A wonderfully insightful series.

The Wanderings I, II, III, IV—20 Audio CDs.

Galatians

Series by John Higgins. Jesus said the truth will make you free. The study of Galatians clarifies the difference between grace and legalism, and frees the believer to be able to serve the Lord with joy.

September 2005. 13 Audio CD Set.

Glorify God

Teaching by John Higgins. Study God's Word daily and your life will be a glorious adventure...if you let Him have His way in your life.

September 2005. Single Audio CD.

James

Teaching by John Higgins. What is being double minded? Find out by studying the Epistle of James—a "How To" book for our Christian Life. James addresses trials, pride, humility, boastfulness, and patience.

May 2006. 24 Studies on 16 Audio CDs.

Israel Tour 2005

This tour includes a Bible Study at each site taught by one of several Pastors including John and Jeremy Higgins, Huck Kusner, and Jim Remington.

March 2005. 4 Video DVDs with worship music. Item 160

Revelation

Series by John Higgins. There is a special blessing to those that study the book of Revelation (1:3). Get a Biblical overview of Revelation by watching this verse-by-verse study.

Summer 2006. 35 Studies on 7 video DVDs.

The Earth Shall Reel

Teaching by John Higgins. Was the earthquake and Tsunami of December 2004 a warning from God and a precursor of His coming judgment? The Sumatra quake actually shook the entire earth's surface.

September 2005. Single Audio CD.

Biblical Studies

Who's Who in the Zoo

Teaching by John Higgins. It's hard to tell the players without a scorecard. *Who's Who in the Zoo* from Genesis 10 sorts out the players in the Middle East, and helps clarify the ongoing conflict from a Biblical perspective.

April 2007. Single study audio CD with maps and chart.

The History of Tomorrow

Series by John Higgins. The History of Tomorrow is a verse-by-verse study from Revelation—The future of the church and world foretold by the Lord Jesus Christ.

September 2005. 6 Audio CDs.

The Rapture

Teaching by John Higgins. Is there a Rapture? Is it in the Bible? When did the teaching emerge? When will it happen? Pre-, Mid-, or Post-tribulation? Not at all? This study addresses these and other questions with solid, scriptural answers.

September 2005. 4 Audio CDs.

The Sacrificing of Truth

Teaching by John Higgins. Is today's "Bible-less" Christianity leading to the strong delusion and lie that is coming on the whole world? This study from Jeremiah explores the standard that defines truth.

September 2005. Single Audio CD.

Spiritual Warfare

Series by John Higgins. The story of the Israelites in Egypt—how God, systematically defeated all of the Egyptian gods. We see behind the scenes in our spiritual battles, and helps us understand Revelation. From Exodus 1.

September 2005. 10 CD set.

Conference Sets

Islam, Israel, and Realty

Is Islam a religion of peace and tolerance? You decide. We are indeed living in perilous times—the world seems to have gone upside down. It's time for believers to look up, for their "redemption draweth nigh."

June 2007. 12 Studies and Q&A on 5 DVDs plus one mp3 Audio CD with all 12 Studies

The Hope That Is Set Before Us

David Hocking, Jacob Prasch, Roger Oakland, Bill Koenig, Roni Simon, and John Higgins speak on our Blessed Hope in these troubled times—the glorious appearing of our great God and our Saviour Jesus Christ!

January 2007. 12 Studies on 6 DVDs, and one mp3 CD with 12 audio studies.

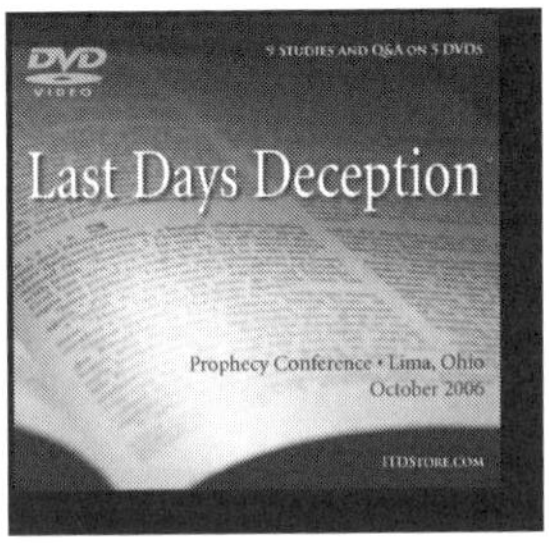

Last Days Deception

Listen to Ed Gaines, Bill Koenig, Roger Oakland, and Mike Spaulding as they speak on Last Days Spiritual Deception, Israel and World Peace, the Emerging Church, Replacement Theology, Marian Apparitions, and Remaining Faithful.

October 2006. 9 Studies and Q&A on 5 DVDs.

Biblical Christianity and Catholicism

Biblical Christianity and Roman Catholicism—what's the difference? Find out in this insightful series taught by Mike Gendron, Roger Oakland, Jacob Prasch, and John Higgins.

June 2005. 10 Studies and Q&A on 7 Video DVDs.

Creation/Evolution

The Biblical account of Creation is of pivotal importance to our faith. Listen to Roger Oakland and Rick Oliver explain why. Includes worship music by the Pearce Family Bluegrass Band.

May 2006. 7 Studies plus Q&A on 5 Video DVDs.

Note: Some album cover artwork may differ from what is pictured.

About John Higgins

Pastor John Higgins, Senior Pastor at Calvary Chapel Tri-City, Tempe, Arizona, has served in the ministry over 38 years. Pastor John had a burden for a generation of hippies and surfers, and was used in the "Jesus movement" of the Holy Spirit to bring thousands of young people to Jesus Christ in the '60s. He's created several websites to spread God's Word, including InTheDays.com that reviews current events in the light of scripture.

Visit these helpful and informative online Biblical resources:

www.TheHistoryOfTomorrow.com
The Manasseh Effect text is available as an Acrobat file for reading, and the companion chart can be downloaded and printed.

www.JesusLifeAndMinistry.com
FREE study of the Life of Christ on DVD in the order the events happened taught by Pastor John.

www.RadioFreeChurch.com
View and listen to archived Biblical messages, Godly Conferences sets, message sets, and Bible School courses. Find what you are looking for by topic or keyword.

www.InTheDays.com
Current news events in the light of Biblical prophecy.

www.GodlyConferences.com
Information about scheduled Christian conferences, focused on expounding and teaching the Word of God. Live Broadcasts.

www.ITDStore.com
Visit the In The Days Bookstore for more studies by Pastor John or to purchase additional copies of *The Manasseh Effect*, as well as selected books and other resources to help you grow in your walk with Jesus!